STANDARD AMERICAN BRIDGE UPDATED

five-card majors

By
Norma Sands

ROCKY MOUNTAIN BOOKS

First Edition, 1980
Second Printing, November, 1980
Third Printing, 1983
Fourth Printing, 1985
Fifth Printing, 1987
Sixth Printing, 1990
Seventh Printing, 1995
Eighth Printing, 1998
Manufactured in the United States of America

ISBN 0-9606548-0-2

Published by
Rocky Mountain Books
Post Office Box 100663
Denver, Colorado 80210

TO
MY FATHER
AND IN MEMORY OF
MY MOTHER

with appreciation to
Sue Edwards, Jan Janitschke, and Paul Ossip

FOREWORD

Bridge is a game of skill and logic that is enjoyed by millions. Like many things that involve interactions of people, bridge has developed a great deal over the years. My purpose in this text is to provide the aspiring bridge player with a bidding structure that reflects current trends. The chapters were planned at a pace suitable for class instruction, which many people find to be an effective and enjoyable way to learn bridge.

Somewhat unique in this text is the addition of five chapters on card play. After digesting the chapters on bidding and card play, the student should have a sound background in all aspects of the game.

Norma Sands

TABLE OF CONTENTS

INTRODUCTION

Bridge is a challenging game that can provide hours and hours of entertainment. Learning to play well requires some effort, but it will be well worth the time spent. It will open up a new world for you by creating a bond with the millions of people who have learned to love the game. You will get to know many people that you might not otherwise have met. In addition to social bridge, there are duplicate bridge clubs and tournaments available in every major city in the country.

The game of bridge consists of a series of hands in which the entire deck of 52 cards is dealt in clockwise rotation to the four players. Each hand consists of two phases, bidding and play. The bidding phase of the hand is frequently referred to as the auction since each bid is higher than the preceding bid until someone "buys" the contract. You bid to describe your hand, listen to what partner bids and communicate information about your hands to know how much you should bid and whether you want to name a certain suit as trump or play without a trump suit. Your partner is the cheerful person across the table from you. After the bidding is complete, the hand is played. The object is to take at least as many tricks as you have bid or "contracted" to take. A trick is completed when a card is played from each hand in clockwise rotation. The hand which plays the highest card of the suit led wins the trick, unless a trump is played. The normal order of high cards exists. The ace is the highest, then the K, Q, J, 10, etc. You must play a card of the suit that is led if you have one, but when there is a trump suit and you have no cards of the suit led, you can capture the trick by playing a trump. For example, if an opponent led the ace of clubs and each hand followed suit with a club, the opponents would win that trick because the ace is always the highest. If, however, you were out of clubs and hearts were trump, you could capture the trick by playing any heart. If more than one hand plays a trump, the highest trump would capture the trick. The fact that there is a trump suit does not mean that you have to trump if you are out of the suit led; you also have the option of discarding an unwanted card of another suit.

There are 13 possible tricks to be taken, since each person is dealt 13 cards. Whichever side takes more than six tricks has taken more than half. For bidding purposes, the number you bid is the number of tricks you hope to take *over six*. The first six tricks taken are referred to as your "book". If a pair has bid to 2♠, spades will be trump and eight or more tricks need to be taken to fulfill the bid (6 + 2). A bid of 3◇ means that diamonds will be trump and nine or more tricks are needed to make the contract. A bid of 1 NT means that there is no trump suit and at least seven tricks are needed. A bid of six would mean 12 tricks need to be taken. This is all but one trick and is called a small slam. A bid of seven, contracting to take all the tricks, is called a grand slam. You get points if you make your contract, but if you fail to take as many tricks as you bid, the opponents will receive penalty points.

One thing that is different about bridge from most other card games, is that there is a rank of the suits for bidding purposes. Clubs is the lowest ranking, then diamonds, hearts, and spades. Notice that they are in alphabetical order. Clubs and diamonds are referred to as the minor suits, and hearts and spades as the major suits. No trump (the absence of a trump suit) is higher ranking than any suit. In bidding, each bid must be higher than the one preceding it. A bid of 1 ◇ would be higher than 1 ♣; a bid of 1 ♠ would be higher than 1 ♣, 1 ◇, or 1 ♡. If someone opened the bidding 1 ◇, anyone at the table could still bid 1 ♡ or 1 ♠ or 1NT (no trump), but if someone wanted to bid clubs, they would need to bid at least 2 ♣, since clubs are lower ranking than diamonds. Over a 1 ♠ opener, someone could still bid 1NT, but any suit bids would have to be at least on the two level. If 1NT has been bid, all the one level bids have been used up. This continues at each level all the way up through the seven level. 7NT is the highest bid that can be made.

The dealer begins the bidding with a pass or with a bid of a suit or no trump. If he thinks his hand is good, he will usually bid something. He can bid anything from one to seven of any suit or no trump. The vast majority of hands, however, are opened on the one level. The idea is to hope partner can bid also, and together to arrive at the best contract.

After the bidding has begun, it proceeds in clockwise rotation, each person having a turn to bid or pass. Once someone has opened the bidding, it continues until there are three consecutive passes. If a person passes at his first turn, he can still bid at a later turn. The last bid determines the final contract. The first person of the partnership to have bid the suit (or no trump) that becomes the final contract, is called the declarer. This person plays both his hand and his partner's, which is spread open-faced on the table and is called the dummy.

Example Auction

North	East	South	West
pass	1 ♥	1 ♠	2 ♥
4 ♠	pass	pass	pass

In this hand, North was the dealer and began the bidding with a pass. The final contract is 4 ♠ by the North-South pair. The South player is the declarer as he started the spades. The person to the left of the declarer makes the opening lead, then the dummy hand is spread on the table.

I

BEGINNING BRIDGE

The first thing to be concerned with in bridge is the bidding. For this you need to have some way of evaluating whether a hand is good, fair or poor. In the 1940's, Charles Goren popularized a method of hand evaluation known as "point count bidding". Point count bidding made bidding easier and more accurate and is now considered standard. This text will use the standard point count bidding and will reflect some of the recent trends that have taken place in bidding. When you have learned this basic material, you should be able to play comfortably with any qualified player anywhere in the country.

Point count bidding assigns value to those cards most likely to take tricks. Aces, the highest card of each suit, are given a value of 4 points, kings 3 points, queens 2 points, and jacks 1 point. These are your *honor count* or your *high card points*. The ten is considered an honor also, but is not given points. Since there are four each of aces, kings, queens, and jacks, there is a total of 40 high card points in the deck. A hand with about ten high card points would be an average hand.

A = 4 points
K = 3 points
Q = 2 points
J = 1 point

In addition to high card points, value is given for short suits in your hand, provided that you are going to bid a suit rather than no trump. A suit containing only two cards, called a doubleton, is given a value of one point, a singleton or a one card suit, a value of 2 points, and a void, or a suit missing from your hand, a value of 3 points. When you have a short suit, you are speculating that one of your longer suits will be selected as a trump suit. If, for example, you were playing with diamonds as trump, and you had only one spade in your hand, your short suit would be useful. The second time spades were played you could capture an opponent's high honor with one of your small trump. These short suit points are referred to as your distributional points. Also, short suits mean corresponding long suits, which can be used to set up tricks.

Doubleton = 1 point
Singleton = 2 points
Void   = 3 points

13 is the number that has been used for many years as the amount of points needed to open the bidding with one of a suit. The following is recommended: count your high card points and consider the distributional points as pluses. An opening hand will usually contain at least 12 or 13 HCP. 11 HCP is acceptable only with a good excuse, such as a long and good suit, as well as some pluses.

> **You may open the bidding with 1NT (notrump) if your hand contains exactly 15, 16, 17, or 18 HCP and is a balanced hand.**

A balanced hand means no singletons or voids and no more than one doubleton.

A brief discussion of scoring is necessary for you to understand the objectives in bidding. The amount of points you receive for making your contract varies depending on what was named as trump. Clubs and diamonds, the minor suits, are worth 20 points for each number you bid and make. For example, a bid of 2♣ would be worth 40 points (2x20) **if you take eight tricks** (six plus the number bid). Hearts and spades, the major suits, are worth 30 points for each number you bid and make. A bid of 3 hearts means that hearts are trump and if you take nine tricks, you would get 90 points (3 x 30). No trump bids work a little differently. The first trick in NT is worth 40 points and all subsequent tricks are worth 30 points. A bid of 2NT making two, eight tricks in all, would be worth 70 points. A bid of 3NT making three, nine tricks, would be worth 100 points.

♣	20 points per trick bid and made
♦	20 points per trick bid and made
♥	30 points per trick bid and made
♠	30 points per trick bid and made
No Trump	40 points first trick, 30 points each subsequent trick bid and made

One of the main objectives in bidding is to bid a game, if your hand plus partner's is good enough. Games are important to bid because large bonus points are added to your score, later, for games bid and made. Bidding game means making a bid that would give you 100 points, or more. A bid of **5♣ or ◊ would be game** (5 x 20). A bid of **4 ♡ or♠ would be game** (4 x 30). Notice that 3♡ or 3♠ would only be 90 (3 x 30). **In NT, a bid of three would be game** (40 + 30 + 30). Notice that in clubs or diamonds you have to bid more to make game than you do in hearts or spades. The major suits are therefore more desirable trump suits than the minors, since you need fewer tricks. If you should make enough tricks for game, but didn't bid it, you don't get credit for the game.

Examples of scores

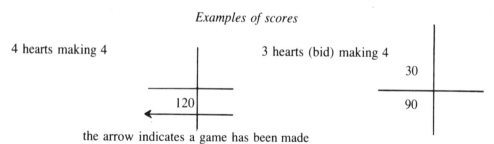

4 hearts making 4

120

3 hearts (bid) making 4

30

90

the arrow indicates a game has been made

You will notice that in the first example a game has been bid and made. In the second example you also made four, but because you only bid 3♡, you do not get credit for the game. The extra trick you took is counted, but you didn't win a game because you didn't bid it. The scores below the line record games or partials (part of games) and above the line record extra tricks, bonuses and penalties incurred by the opponents. See page 79.

You may wonder at this point, how you can ever know if the combined hands are good enough for game. A guide line is that if it can be determined, through the bidding, that the two hands contain a total of 26 points, game should be bid, as **26 points will normally produce game.** A bit more may be needed if a minor suit is selected as trump, because an additional trick is needed in order to make a game. For future reference, 33 points will usually produce a small slam, and 37 points, a grand slam.

Let's look at an example where you could know that your partnership has enough points for game. Your partner has opened 1NT and you have

♠ A 6 5
♥ 6 5
♦ A 7 6 5
♣ K 8 7 6

Your partner has announced 15-18 high-card points, and you have 11 high-card points. There is a total of 26 + points between the two hands. *You* know that there are enough points for game, so *you* should bid 3NT.

When partner has opened 1NT, if you are *willing* to play in a NT contract, with

0-7   high card points, pass, as the partnership cannot have enough points for game.

8-9   high card points, bid 2NT. This invites partner to bid game (3NT) if he has the top of his bid (17 or 18 points).

10-14 high card points, bid 3NT. True, if partner has only 15, you may be on 25 points, but when you know you are, *at worst*, within one point of game, that's close enough.

A SAMPLE HAND FOR YOU TO PRACTICE AT HOME.

THE AUCTION

you			
South	West	North	East
1NT	pass	3NT	pass
pass	pass		

North
♠ A 4 3
♥ K 6 3
♦ 8 7 6 5
♣ K 5 4

West
♠ Q J 2
♥ Q 10 7 4 2
♦ A 3 2
♣ 3 2

East
♠ 10 9 8 7
♥ J 9 8
♦ 9 4
♣ Q J 10 9

South
♠ K 6 5
♥ A 5
♦ K Q J 10
♣ A 8 7 6

You, as south, first bid the NT, so you are declarer. Your left hand opponent is on lead and leads a low heart. (His normal lead is the 4 of hearts, the fourth card down from his longest suit.) Partner's hand (North) is spread on the table. By looking at the two hands, you see you have two top spade winners, the A and K, two top hearts, the A and K, and the same in clubs. This makes six tricks you can easily win, but you need nine tricks to make 3NT. You can easily come to three diamond tricks, if you are willing to lose a trick. Since this is a sure way to take nine tricks, you should lead a diamond as soon as you win the opening heart trick, while you still have your high cards in the other suits. As you are playing the hand, whichever hand wins a trick is the first hand to play to the next trick.

QUIZ ON INTRODUCTION AND BEGINNING BRIDGE

1. To open the bidding with one of a suit you need____points.
2. To open the bidding with 1NT, you need____,____,____, or____high card points.
3. A bid of two means you have to take____tricks.
4. A bid of six is called a____ ____and you need to take____tricks.
5. The most you can bid in bridge is____.
6. Your distribution points count a doubleton as____, a singleton as____ and a void as____.
7. There are____high card points in a full deck.
8. An ace is____points, a king____, a queen____, and a jack is____point.
9. Game means getting at least____points below the line.
10. A bid of____of a minor suit will produce a game.
11. A bid of____of hearts or spades will produce a game.
12. A bid of____NT will produce a game.
13. If a partnership owns a total of____points, a game should be bid because it's likely to be made.
14. A bid of 3♠ making four is____points below the line and____points above the line.
15. A bid of 1NT making one is____points.
16. A bid of 4◇ making four is____points.
17. In scoring, the points for extra tricks, bonuses and opponents' penalties go____the line. Game points are written____the line.
18. If you fail to make your contract, your opponents will receive____points.

Answers:

1. 13	10. 5
2. 15, 16, 17, 18	11. 4
3. 8	12. 3
4. Small slam 12	13. 26
5. 7	14. 90 30
6. 1, 2, 3	15. 40
7. 40	16. 80
8. 4, 3, 2, 1	17. Above below
9. 100	18. Penalty

II

OPENING BIDS

You may open the bidding with any bid from one to seven. The vast majority of hands that you open will be one of a suit or 1NT. This gives your partner an opportunity to tell you about his hand. Often there are several bids taken before there is enough information passed to know what, if anything, should be trump, and if it should be bid to a game or a slam. It may become clear that there aren't enough points to be bid that high. In that case, you will end the bidding at some low level and attempt to get a part of a game, which is called a "partial". You may have an opportunity to complete your game on the next hand. As a note of reminder, in bridge the order of suits is ♣ ◇ ♡ ♠ NT. Spades is the highest ranking suit for bidding purposes, but no trump is higher than any suit.

We have already learned about an opening bid of 1NT. Opening bids of one of a suit are made on a great variety of hands. The point count for opening one of a suit is 13 to about 22. Hands in excess of this are usually opened on the two level. Remember in suit bidding we count our high card points and consider our distribution as well. *All hands with 13 high card points should be opened and most hands with 12 HCP should be opened if there are any distribution points. Hands with 11 HCP plus two for distribution may be opened if there is a long-strong suit.* After determining if we have enough points to bid, the next decision is which suit to bid. If the hand contains one long suit (five cards or more), the decision is easy. You simply bid one of your long suit, even if you have a shorter suit that is stronger. In attempting to determine if the hand should be played with a trump suit, length is what is important. If a hand is played with a particular suit as trump, the partnership should, in general, hold at least eight cards of the suit. When you and your partner have eight cards of a particular suit and the opponents have five, you have a considerable advantage. If you hold a spade suit of AKQJ and partner has 987 in spades, and you have a heart suit with 98765 and a partner has 10432, hearts should most definitely be trumps. The partnership has nine hearts and only seven spades. The high heart honors will be losers regardless of which suit is selected as trump.

The style of bidding known as five-card majors has become so popular that it is considered standard. This means that the opening bidder needs to have at least five hearts or spades in order to open with 1♡ or 1♠. Any hand that is good enough to open and does not have five hearts or five spades is opened the longer of the two minor suits. Notice that this might mean opening a three card minor suit. For example, if you have four spades, four hearts, three diamonds and two clubs, you would open the hand 1◇. Opening the bidding with one of a minor is one of the *rare* occasions in bridge when it's acceptable to bid a three-card suit. **If you have points enough to open the bidding with one of a suit and have no five-card major, with three clubs and three diamonds open 1♣, with four clubs and four diamonds, open 1◇.** Although it is acceptable to open the bidding with a three-card minor, **it should be noted that an opening bid of 1♣ or 1◇ will typically be made with four or more cards in the suit.** One advantage of using the five card major style of bidding is that when your partner opens with 1♠, for example, and you have three or more spades, you *know* you have located a trump suit which is playable. Together you have eight or more cards in the suit. Now your job is simply to determine if the cards are good enough to bid a game or possibly a slam.

One further note regarding opening bids: if, as opening bidder, you hold two five-card suits, you bid the *higher ranking* suit first. If your partner does not support that suit, you will bid your second five-card suit at your next bid.

In addition to the point count guidelines we have already learned, deductions need to be made for "unguarded" honors. The reason for this is, for example, a singleton King is a "goner" if the ace of that suit is led. It is still better than a small card, however, as partner could have the ace or the queen. If you have an unguarded honor of a K, Q, or J, deduct one point.

If you hold a singleton or doubleton in a suit, your point count would be as follows:

high card + distribution

A	=	4	+	2	(the ace needs no extra card or guard)
K	=	2	+	2	
Q	=	1	+	2	
J	=	0	+	2	
K2	=	3	+	1	(one card is a sufficient guard for a king)
Q6	=	1	+	1	
J5	=	0	+	1	

You are the dealer and you have the following hands. Practice counting your points and determining your opening bid.

1. ♠ A K 7 6
   ♥ Q 8 7 6
   ♦ 10 8 7
   ♣ A 5

2. ♠ 10 7 6 5 4
   ♥ A K 5 3
   ♦ A Q 4
   ♣ 7

3. ♠ A K 8 7
   ♥ A 8 7
   ♦ A 8 7
   ♣ Q 4 3

4. ♠ A K 8 7 6
   ♥ Q 8 7
   ♦ 9 8 7
   ♣ Q 8

5. ♠ 8 7 4
   ♥ A 8 7 6
   ♦ A 7 6
   ♣ A Q 7

6. ♠ Q 8 7 6 2
   ♥ A J 8 7 6
   ♦ A 8
   ♣ A

7. ♠ A 8
   ♥ 9 5 3
   ♦ K Q 7 3
   ♣ K Q 9 8

8. ♠ K
   ♥ Q J 6 5 4
   ♦ A K 4 2
   ♣ 8 7 6

1. You have 13 high-card points and one doubleton. 1 ♦ should be your bid. This is your better minor suit, because you have more of them. If your length in the minors is unequal, bid the longer. Remember you can't open a four card major.

2. Your point count is 13 in high cards plus 2 for distribution. You have a five card suit; bid it. 1♠.
3. Open with 1NT. This hand has 17 high-card points and is balanced.
4. Pass. The spade suit is good and five long, but this hand doesn't have the points to open, 11 high cards minus 1 for the unguarded club honor plus 1 for the doubleton makes a total of 11.
5. You have 14 HCP, but no five-card major. Open 1♣.
6. You have 15 HCP and 3 in distribution. Open 1♠. With two five-card suits, open the higher ranking.
7. You have 14 HCP and 1 point for distribution. With two four-card minors, open the higher ranking. Bid 1◇.
8. This hand has 13 HCP minus one for the unguarded king. 12 plus 2 should be opened. Bid 1♡.

Practice this hand by laying out all four hands. The dealer is the first to begin the bidding. The dealer is usually determined on the first hand by drawing for the highest card. From then on, the deal rotates clockwise around the table.

North
♠ A Q 2
♥ 7 6 5
♦ 7 6 5 4
♣ A 4 3

West
♠ K 9 4
♥ 10 4 2
♦ 10 2
♣ Q 10 8 7 6

East
♠ J 7 5
♥ K Q J 9
♦ J 9 8
♣ J 9 2

South - Declarer
♠ 10 8 6 3
♥ A 8 3
♦ A K Q 3
♣ K 5

THE AUCTION

East	South	West	North
pass	1NT	pass	3NT
pass	pass	pass	

South is the declarer. The 7 of clubs is led (fourth down from the longest suit). Pretend you are South, the declarer. Count your top tricks. There are seven—one spade, one heart, three diamonds, and two clubs. You need nine tricks to make your contract. There are usually possible tricks to be found in addition to the top tricks. In this hand, the diamond suit has a total of eight cards. The opponents have only five. If those cards are three in one hand and two in the other, the last small diamond played by declarer will be a winner. In the spade suit, if you lead from your hand towards the AQ, and West plays low, play the Q. This is called a finesse. You will win the trick if West has the K and didn't play it. If instead, West plays his K, it's easy. Win the A and your Q is good. You should win the opening club lead with the K in your hand. Since you know that you need to play a spade toward the AQ for a finesse, do it now. If the K is located where you want it to be, you are likely to make your contract. It is important to start developing your possible tricks early in a hand.

QUIZ ON OPENING BIDS

1. If you have____or more points, you may open the bidding with one of a suit.
2. An opening bid of one heart or one spade shows no less than____cards in that suit.
3. A balanced hand of 15, 16, 17 or 18 high card points is opened with____.
4. ____is the highest ranking suit.
5. The minor suits are____and____.
6. The major suits are____and____.

True or False
7. It is acceptable to open the bidding with 1♣ or 1♢ on a three-card suit.____
8. It is acceptable to open the bidding with 1♣ or 1♢ on a two-card suit.____
9. If someone at the table has bid 1 heart and you want to bid your diamond suit, you must bid at least 2♢.____

You are the dealer. What do you bid with each of the following hands.

10. ♠ A K 4 3
    ♥ A 4 3 2
    ♦ 3 2
    ♣ K 7 6

11. ♠ K 7 6 5
    ♥ K 4 3 2
    ♦ A 3 2
    ♣ 4 3

12. ♠ 7 6 5 4 3
    ♥ A K 4 3
    ♦ A 2
    ♣ K 2

13. ♠ A Q 2
    ♥ 4 3
    ♦ A 7 6 4
    ♣ A K 4 3

14. ♠ A 5 4 3
    ♥ K Q 6 5
    ♦ J 8 6
    ♣ A 2

15. ♠ J 8 4 3 2
    ♥ A 9 8 6 4
    ♦ A K
    ♣ 2

16. ♠ A Q 5 4 2
    ♥ 3
    ♦ A K J 8 4 2
    ♣ 9

Answers:

1. 13
2. 5
3. 1NT
4. Spades
5. Clubs, diamonds
6. Hearts, spades
7. True
8. False
9. True
10. 1♣, your longer minor
11. Pass
12. 1♥, your five-card suit
13. 1NT
14. 1♢
15. 1♥, with two five-card suits, bid the higher ranking.
16. 1♢, you have five spades, but six diamonds.

III

RESPONDING TO PARTNER'S OPENING BID OF ONE OF A SUIT BY RAISING HIS SUIT

Your choices of responses to your partner's opening bid of one of a suit are basically raising his suit, bidding a suit of your own, or bidding NT. **Any time your hand contains 6 or more points, you should find some response, as partner's hand could be big enough for game opposite your 6 points.** With less than 6 points, you should pass.

A very broad generalization of priorities between bidding your own suit or raising partner's is as follows:

Raise your partner's MAJOR suit with three or more cards in that suit. Since he has at least five when he opens a major, with three or more in your hand, the partnership has at least *eight*, which is enough for a trump suit.

Bid your own suit (four or more cards) over partner's 1♣ or 1♦ opening. At your first response you should have five or more of partner's minor suit to raise it. Although partner will usually have more than a three-card suit, minors produce the lowest scores and so become our last choice.

If you decide to raise partner's suit, your point count determines how high to raise. NOTE: WHEN YOU DISCOVER A TRUMP FIT WITH PARTNER, YOUR DISTRIBUTION IS KNOWN TO BE WORKING, SO THOSE POINTS COUNT **FULL** VALUE. A DOUBLETON IS 1 POINT, A SINGLETON IS NOW PROMOTED FROM 2 TO 3 POINTS, AND A VOID FROM 3 TO 5 POINTS. THIS IS VALID WHEN YOU HAVE 4+ TRUMPS FOR YOUR RAISE.

Raising partner's suit from one to two shows 6-10 points including distribution. If partner opens 1♥, bid 2♥ with each of the following.

♠	A 8 7 2	♠	8 7 6	♠	2
♥	Q 6 5	♥	8 7 2	♥	9 8 3 2
♦	9 8 5 4	♦	A J 7 6	♦	A 4 3 2
♣	3 2	♣	A 8 4	♣	6 5 3 2

Raising a minor suit requires more trumps. Partner opens 1♦. Raise to 2♦ with

♠	6 4 3	♠	3 2
♥	3	♥	6 2
♦	A J 6 5 3	♦	J 9 6 4 2
♣	J 5 4 2	♣	A 7 5 2

Notice that there is no four-card or longer major suit to bid. That would be our first priority because major suits count more.

Raising partner's suit from one to three shows 13 to 16 points, including distribution, and is forcing at least to game.

26 points are needed for game, and the bidding has shown a combined count of 26 or more. If partner opens 1♠, raise to 3♠ on the following:

♠ 9 8 6 2   ♠ K 4 3 2
♥ 4   ♥ A 7 5
♦ A 8 6 2   ♦ Q 7 2
♣ A K 8 2   ♣ A 7 5

Raising a partner's suit directly to game shows a hand that is rather weak in terms of high cards, but is a super fitting hand. It should contain at least five trumps, an outside singleton or void, about 6 HCP, give or take a couple. For example, if partner opens 1♠, bid 4♠ with

♠ K 9 8 6 2
♥ — — —
♦ Q 8 6 3
♣ 8 6 3 2

With partner bidding 1♠,
this hand becomes a
Magic Hand

If it doesn't make, it will probably prevent the opponents from being able to find their heart game.

If you want to raise partner's suit, but have 11-12 points, you need to temporize by bidding a suit of your own first, then give an encouraging raise of partner's suit at your second bid.

Sample hand to practice

North
♠ K 3
♥ Q 4 3 2
♦ A K 3 2
♣ 9 5 4

West
♠ A 8 5 2
♥ J 10 9
♦ 5
♣ Q 10 8 7 6

East
♠ 10 9 7 6 4
♥ 5
♦ 10 9 8 7
♣ A K J

South
♠ Q J
♥ A K 8 7 6
♦ Q J 6 4
♣ 3 2

An opening lead is made of the 5 of diamonds against a contract of 4♡ by the North-South pair. West is hoping partner can win the opening lead or some early trick and return a diamond, so he can trump it. Declarer, on this hand, must play trump immediately to remove all trump from the opponents' hands. Declarer will lose only the ace of spades and two club tricks, since he can trump any further club leads. He will lose three tricks and take the rest, which is 10 tricks, making 4♡. If he fails to pull trump, he could get one of his diamonds trumped and lose too many tricks.

QUIZ

1. With____or more points, you should find some response to partner's opening bid of 1 of a suit.
2. You need to have____or more cards of partner's minor to raise at your first opportunity.
3. You need to have____or more cards of partner's major to raise at your first opportunity.
4. Raising partner's suit from 1 to 2 shows____to____points.
5. A singleton is worth____points when raising partner's suit, and a void is worth ____points when raising partner's suit.
6. A raise of partner's suit from 1 to 3 is____. (forcing or non-forcing)

Partner opens 1♡ and you have the following. What is your bid?

7. ♠ A 8 7 6 2		8. ♠ A Q 7 4		9. ♠ 7 6 4 3		
♥ A 7 6		♥ 7 6 5 2		♥ A Q 5 4		
♦ 8 7 2		♦ A K		♦ A Q 4 2		
♣ 4 3		♣ 10 9 3		♣ 2		

10. ♠ — — —		11. ♠ 8 7 4		12. ♠ 6 5 4		
♥ K 8 7 6 2		♥ A 6 5		♥ 8 7 6		
♦ Q J 6 2		♦ 7 6 4 2		♦ A Q 8 7 6		
♣ 8 7 6 2		♣ 7 6 2		♣ 3 2		

Answers:

1. 6
2. 5
3. 3
4. 6-10
5. 3, 5
6. Forcing
7. 2♡
8. 3♡
9. 3♡
10. 4♡
11. Pass
12. 2♡

IV

RESPONDING TO ONE OF A SUIT BY BIDDING A NEW SUIT OR NO TRUMP

When you are considering bidding a suit of your own over partner's opening bid of one of a suit, pay the most attention to your high-card points. *Do not* add value for shortness in partner's suit. You may count it later if you and partner agree on a different trump suit. ***Responding*** *with a suit of your own on the one level such as (1♣—1♡) shows at least four cards of the suit you bid and 6-18 points, possibly more.* Notice that this is a very wide range. It is therefore forcing on partner to bid again, because if you happen to have a very big hand, you will want to bid a game, even possibly a slam.

In auctions involving suit bidding,

> **A new suit by responder is forcing.**

Once again, the one-over-one bid shows at least 6 points and could be a very big hand. If partner opens one of a minor and you have any four-card or longer major suit, you should bid it, assuming you have at least 6 points. (Occasionally you may have a longer minor suit which you choose to bid first. This would require two bids so tends to indicate a good hand.) **If you have four hearts and four spades, respond with 1♡.** If a partner has four hearts, he will raise your hearts immediately. If not, he will bid a four-card spade suit, if he has it. You will find out very early in the bidding if you have a major suit fit. **If you have five hearts and five spades, respond 1♠.** If partner doesn't raise your spades, you will next bid hearts. **Anytime in bridge when you have five hearts and five spades, you should bid spades first.** However, if the bidding were to go: 1♢—1♠—2♢—2♡, responder has shown five spades and four hearts. With two five card suits, he would have to bid hearts again to complete the picture.

Responding with a suit of your own on the two level, called a two-over-one bid, shows a fairly good hand, or possibly a very good hand. It should describe a hand of 10 high card points, at a minimum, and four or more cards of the suit you bid. This occurs when the suit you want to bid is lower ranking than the suit your partner opened. Examples: 1♡—2♣, 1♠—2♢, 1♢—2♣. This bid is forcing on partner to bid again also, because although your hand could contain as few as ten points, it could also be as big as 18+ points.

Responding with a deliberate jump of one level (1♢—2♠, 1♡—3♣) is a super hand, 19 or more points. This jump shows a hand so big that game is guaranteed and slam must be considered. The suit in which you are jumping should be at least five-cards long.

---

*Throughout this text, a dash between two bids indicates a pass by the next player.

THE BIDS JUST DESCRIBED NEED TO BE UNDERSTOOD THOROUGHLY. READ THE LAST THREE PARAGRAPHS OVER SEVERAL TIMES UNTIL YOU ARE SURE OF THEM.

This leads to the 1NT response. **A 1NT response shows a hand of 6-10 high card points, denies having a four-card or longer heart or spade suit that could be bid at the one level, and if partner has opened a heart or a spade, it denies holding three or more cards of his major suit.** The 1NT response does *not* necessarily show a balanced hand.

When partner has opened one of a suit, a response of 2NT is made with a balanced hand of 13-15 high card points. A response of 3NT is made with a balanced hand of 16-18 high card points. These bids should not be in preference to bidding your four-card major suit, if you can do so on the one level, and they tend to deny having as many as three cards of partner's major suit. It is therefore usually a 4-4-3-2 distribution, since we normally will bid our five-card suit.

Plan your responses to the following bids, given the following hands. *Remember with 6 points, you should find something to bid.*

Partner opened 1 ♦
1. ♠ Q 8 6 2
   ♥ A 7
   ♦ 9 7 4
   ♣ J 8 6 3

Partner opened 1 ♣
2. ♠ 5 3 2
   ♥ A 6 4
   ♦ K 6 4
   ♣ J 9 7 3

Partner opened 1 ♠
3. ♠ 8 6
   ♥ 6 3
   ♦ A Q 8 6 3
   ♣ J 9 7 2

Partner opened 1 ♥
4. ♠ A 4
   ♥ 9 6 2
   ♦ J 8 6 2
   ♣ K 8 6 3

1. You should bid 1 ♠. Your partner could have four spades, so you could have a spade fit (eight or more cards between the two hands is enough to have a trump suit). If you respond with 1NT, you would be telling your partner that you don't have either four hearts or four spades.

2. Respond with 1NT. You do have four of partner's clubs, but as a first response, you should have five cards to raise partner's minor suit.

3. Bid 1NT. You would like to bid your diamond suit, but your hand isn't good enough. If partner had opened 1 ♣, you could bid 1 ♢, but partner opened 1 ♠. You need 10 HCP to bid a new suit of your own on the two level. If you missed this one, re-read the paragraph on two-over-one bids.

4. Raise to two hearts. This is *not* a two-over-one response. This is simply *raising* partner's suit and is shows 6-10 points including distribution. You should raise partner's suit instead of bidding NT, because partner shows at least five when opening with one heart or one spade. Again, the partnership is known to have at least eight hearts, so that should be trump. You make partner's job easy. He now knows that the hand should be played in hearts. All he has to do now is decide if his hand is good enough to be in game or not.

North
♠ A J 6 5
♥ A 2
♦ 9 8 7
♣ Q J 4 3

West
♠ Q 8 7
♥ 9 8 6 5
♦ A K Q
♣ 10 9 8

East
♠ 10 9
♥ Q J 10 7 4
♦ J 10 3 2
♣ 7 2

South
♠ K 4 3 2
♥ K 3
♦ 6 5 4
♣ A K 6 5

THE AUCTION

North	*East*	*South*	*West*
1♣	pass	1♠	pass
2♠	pass	4♠	pass
pass	pass		

AN OPENING HAND OPPOSITE AN OPENING HAND BELONGS IN GAME.

The opponents begin by taking the K, Q, and A of diamonds, followed by a heart which you win in your hand. You are now "booked," which means that you can't lose any more tricks and still make your contract. The only problem is a possible trump loser. You play the K and then lead towards your AJ6. If your left had opponent plays small, and he should, you play the J. (If you don't do this and instead play the A at the second lead of trump, odds are against East having the lone trump Q at this point.) Now play the A and all the trumps will be removed from the opponents' hands. The rest is easy.

1. Any time you have ___ or more points, you should find some response when partner opens the bidding with one of a suit.
2. A two-over-one bid shows a minimum of ___ high card points.
3. A 1NT response shows ___-___ high card points.
4. A jump shift shows ___ or more points.
5. If partner opens with 1♣ and you have enough points to bid, with five hearts and five spades, you should bid ___ first.
6. If partner opens with 1♣ and you have enough points to bid, with 4 hearts and 4 spades, you should bid ___ first.
7. A response of 2NT shows ___ to ___ high card points.
8. A response of 3NT shows ___ to ___ high card points.

Partner opens 1♢. What is your first response with each of the following hands?

9.   ♠ 9 8 7 5 3
    ♥ A K 7 6
    ♦ 8 7
    ♣ 6 5

10. ♠ A Q 7 6
    ♥ K 7 6 5
    ♦ 8 7
    ♣ 8 7 6

11. ♠ A 7 6 5 3
    ♥ A K 8 7 6
    ♦ K 4
    ♣ 2

12. ♠ A K 5 4 3
    ♥ A 2
    ♦ A 2
    ♣ K 7 6 5

13. ♠ 7 6 5
    ♥ 6 5
    ♦ 8 6 2
    ♣ A Q J 4 3

14. ♠ A 4 3
    ♥ K 6 5
    ♦ K 5 3
    ♣ A 10 7 5

15. ♠ 4 3
    ♥ Q 6 5 4
    ♦ Q 6 5 3
    ♣ K 5 3

Answers:

1. 6
2. 10
3. 6-10
4. 19
5. Spades
6. Hearts
7. 13-15
8. 16-18
9. 1♥
10. 1♥
11. 1♥
12. 2♥
13. 1NT
14. 2NT
15. 1♥

V

SECOND BIDS—BY OPENER

Once the bidding has been opened and partner has responded, opener should clarify the size of his hand with his rebid if possible. Sometimes you won't know, at this point, where the hand should be played, but other times it will be clear to you that a trump suit has been found (eight or more).

If you opened
- ♠ A 4 3 2
- ♥ A 2
- ♦ A J 3 2
- ♣ 7 6 5

with 1◇ and partner responded 1♠, you should raise to 2♠. It's important to set the trump suit early. Partner must have at least four spades, so you know you have eight or more between you. A minimum opening hand is a hand of 13-16 points. You have a minimum hand so you raise a minimum level. REMEMBER THAT A PASS CANNOT BE CONSIDERED AS PARTNER'S HAND COULD BE BIG ENOUGH FOR GAME OR EVEN SLAM.

If you have
- ♠ A 2
- ♥ A J 5 4 3 2
- ♦ K 3 2
- ♣ 4 3

and your partner responds 1♠ to your 1♡ opening bid, your rebid should be 2♡. Rebidding the suit shows a minimum opener, 13-16, and suggests *more* than a five-card suit.

If you opened 1◇ with
- ♠ A 2
- ♥ K 9 3
- ♦ K Q 3 2
- ♣ J 7 6 5

and partner responded 1♠, you should rebid 1NT. This shows a balanced hand that has fewer points than the opening NT range. It pinpoints your range to 12, 13 or 14 high-card points. You could have bid 2♣, your other four-card suit, but 1NT is more descriptive. A rebid of 2◇ should not be considered; **an unsupported 4-card suit is never rebid in bridge.**

Opener can jump a level of bidding to show bigger than minimum hands. If opener jumps to a new suit, called a jump shift, it shows 19+ points.

There are different jumps available to opener. He can jump in his own suit, he can jump in partner's suit, he can jump in notrump, or as indicated above, he can jump in a new suit.

> **Any time opener jumps at his second turn, it shows some kind of strong hand (better than minimum.)**

WHEN REBIDDING, IF YOU KNOW WHERE A HAND SHOULD BE PLAYED AND YOU HAVE ENOUGH POINTS FOR GAME, BID IT.

If you open 1 ♡ with

♠ A 3
♥ A J 6 5 4
♦ A K Q 5
♣ 8 7

and partner raises you to 2 ♡, bid 4 ♡. The trump suit has been set and partner has 6-10 points. Even if partner has only 6 points, with your 20 there are enough for game.

With some hands you will know that there are not enough points for game, so you will want to stop at a low level. If you open 1 ♡ with

♠ A 5
♥ A K 7 6 5
♦ J 8 2
♣ 6 5 4

and partner raises you to 2 ♡, you should pass. Partner has 6-10 points and you have 13, so there are at best 23 points between the two hands. Unless you are hopeful of being in game, there is no point in bidding any higher than necessary.

With some hands, you may have enough points for game, but you can't be sure. You open 1 ♠ with

♠ A J 8 6 4
♥ A K 5 4
♦ K 5
♣ 3 2

and your partner raises you to 2 ♠. You have found a trump suit; your problem on this hand is to determine whether or not there are enough points for game. You have 17 points. If partner has 6-7, game should not be bid; but if partner has 9-10, you would want to be in game. Bid 3 ♠. This gives the decision to partner. If he has 6-7 points, he passes, with 9-10 he should accept your game invitation, by bidding 4 ♠, and if he should happen to be in the middle of his range, 8 points, he will have to use his judgement.

North
♠ K 5
♥ A Q 3 2
♦ K J 3 2
♣ 8 6 2

West
♠ A 9 8 7
♥ 10 9
♦ 7 6
♣ K Q J 7 5

East
♠ Q J 10 6 2
♥ K 8
♦ 10 5 4
♣ 10 9 4

South
♠ 4 3
♥ J 7 6 5 4
♦ A Q 9 8
♣ A 3

THE AUCTION

South	West	North	East
	pass	1 ♦	pass
1 ♥	pass	' 2 ♥	pass
4 ♥	pass	pass	pass

Notice the South hand bids game at the second turn, as the hand has 13 points with distribution.

West leads the club K. (For explanation see Chapter XIII.) You win with the A and play a low heart. When your left hand opponent plays low, you finesse the Q. Unfortunately, it loses to the K. Back comes a club, which is won by the J. The club Q is continued, which you trump in your hand. You now play another heart to your A, which picks up all of the outstanding trumps. How do you play the rest of the hand?

You have lost two tricks. You will need to come back to your hand with a diamond and play a low spade to your K, hoping the A is on your left. You can afford only one more loser. If LHO plays low on your spade lead, play the K.

SECOND BIDS—BY RESPONDER

When responder has bid a new suit at the one level, it shows at least four cards of the suit bid and 6-18 points. Since this is anything from a weak hand to a very good hand, responder's second bid must be carefully selected.

As responder, a minimum rebid of your own suit (if partner hasn't raised it) shows less than an opening hand and usually a six-card suit. The general rule is that if opener rebids NT, responder can rebid a five-card suit, but if opener rebids his own suit or changes suits, responder should have six cards to rebid his own suit. If you have

♠ 7 6
♥ A Q J 4 3 2
♦ 6 5
♣ 4 3 2

and you responded 1 ♡ over partner's 1 ◇ opening, if partner rebids 2 ♣, you should rebid 2 ♡. Often with only 7 points you would pass at your second turn. However, your heart suit is good and you have little support for either of partner's suits.

At your second response, a raise of partner's suit, or NT bids below the game level also show less than an opening hand. If you have

♠ A 4
♥ A 6 5 4
◆ 6 5 4
♣ 8 6 4 2

and partner opened with 1 ◇, you would respond with 1 ♡. If partner next bid 1 ♠, you should bid 1NT. You don't want to pass as partner presumably has only four spades, (with five he would have opened 1 ♠) and you have only two spades. Your 1NT bid shows 6-10 high card-points.

If partner opens 1 ♡ and you have

♠ A 6 5 4
♥ 8 7
◆ K 9 7 6
♣ 8 7 6

you would bid 1 ♠. If partner rebids 2 ♡ you should pass. Partner has a long heart suit and a minimum hand.

If, at your second turn as responder, you have a good hand but don't know where the hand should be played, you can force partner to bid again by bidding a new suit. A new suit by responder is forcing when NT has not been bid. If you have

♠ A Q 5 4 3
♥ A K 5 4
◆ 2
♣ 6 4 2

and partner opened 1 ◇, you bid 1 ♠, and partner rebids 2 ◇, what do you bid? You have an opening hand so you will want to be in game. AN OPENING HAND OPPOSITE AN OPENING HAND BELONGS IN GAME SOMEWHERE. The problem in this hand is you still don't know where; spades, hearts or NT seem most likely. You next bid 2 ♡, which partner cannot pass. If he has four hearts, he should raise hearts. If he has three spades, he should raise spades. (He has already denied having four spades, when he didn't raise them immediately.) If he has neither of these, he would bid NT, if he has some honors in clubs. If he bids 2NT, you bid 3NT.

Very often, however, you will know where the hand should be played when it's time for your second bid. Then your job is to keep the bidding at a low level with weak hands, invite a game with middle-of-the-road hands, or bid game with enough count for game. Occasionally, of course, you will even try for a slam.

If partner opened 1 ◇ and you have

♠ A 8 4 3
♥ K 8 7 5
◆ 4
♣ A Q 5 4

bid 1 ♡. With four hearts and four spades, respond with 1 ♡, regardless of quality. If partner rebids 1 ♠, bid 4 ♠. Partner must have a four-card spade suit, which gives you eight spades. It is your second turn to bid, you have an opening hand and you know what suit should be trumps. Bid the game!!

1. If opener rebids his own suit, it shows a minimum hand of____to____points.
2. If opener raises partner's suit from 1 to 2 (1♣—1♡—2♡) it shows from____ to____points.
3. If opener rebids 1NT, it shows____to____high-card points.
4. A rebid of a suit without a raise from partner always shows at least____cards of the suit.
5. An opening hand opposite an opening hand should be in____somewhere.
6. If responder has an opening hand, at his second turn he must either bid game or make a____bid.

Your partner has opened 1♣. You respond 1♡. Partner rebids 1♠. Plan your next bid with each of these hands.

7. ♠ A 4 3 2   8. ♠ 4 3   9. ♠ A 4 3 2
    ♥ Q 4 3 2   ♥ A K 7 6 3 2   ♥ Q 9 5 3
    ♦ A 4 3   ♦ 8 7 2   ♦ Q 2
    ♣ A 2   ♣ 9 8   ♣ K 3 2

Your partner has opened 1♠. You respond 2♣. Partner rebids 2♡. Plan your next bid with each of these hands.

10. ♠ 3 2   11. ♠ 5 4
    ♥ A 4 3 2   ♥ 6 5
    ♦ 3 2   ♦ A K 4 3
    ♣ A K Q 4 3   ♣ A Q 4 3 2

12. ♠ 4 3
    ♥ Q 2
    ♦ 8 7 6
    ♣ A K Q 4 3 2

Answers:

1. 13-16
2. 13-16
3. 12-14
4. 5. Frequently 6 cards.
5. Game
6. Forcing
7. 4♥. You have an opening hand and it's your second turn.
8. 2♡.
9. 3♥. Near opener
10. 4♥. You have an opening hand and it's your second turn.
11. 3 NT. You have an opening hand and it's your second turn.
12. 3♣. If partner now bids 3NT, you should pass.

VI

OPENING WITH LARGE HANDS

Occasionally you pick up a hand that is so good that you feel you want to be in game even though partner's hand may not be good enough to make a simple response if you were to open one of a suit. These hands are opened with two of a suit. This is a game forcing bid. There are several reasons why you don't simply open the bidding with a game bid with a very large hand. One is that if you leave some bidding space for partner, you may find that he has just what you need for slam. Another is that very often you need partner's help in determining the best game contract.

If you picked up   ♠   A   K   5   4   3
                   ♥   A   K   6   5   4
                   ♦   A   K   J
                   ♣   —   —   —

you have 25 points in your own little paw. It would be sad to have to guess at the best game contract and guess wrong. Open with 2♠. If partner doesn't raise spades, you'll try hearts next.

An opening bid of two of a suit is made with a hand that you can count enough tricks for a game or within one trick of game, or a hand that has about 23 or more points. The hand could be big enough that there is a slam in the hand. The suit bid should have five or more cards.

1.   ♠   A   K   Q   6   5   4   2   2.   ♠   A   Q   J
    ♥   A   K   3   2   ♥   A   K   7   4   2
    ♦   2   ♦   A   Q   J   2
    ♣   3   ♣   2

3.   ♠   A   K   7   4   3   2
    ♥   A   K   Q   J   3
    ♦   A   2
    ♣   —   —   —

1. Open with 2♠. There are probably seven spade tricks and two sure heart tricks. If partner were to have as little as the J10 of hearts and one spade in his hand, a four spade contract is favored to make. An opening bid of 4♠ is saved for hands with a very long suit, such as an eight-card suit, with very few high-cards outside the trump suit.

2. Open with 2♥. You have a 23 point hand. There is too much of a chance that partner has enough for you to make a game somewhere without having enough points to bid over a 1♥ opening.

3. Bid 2♠. Never lose sight of the fact that partner can't pass. If partner should raise your spades, you would want to be in slam. If partner has three or more spades, you

rate to lose one or no spades as the opponents have so few. You have a likely 12 tricks with nothing but a few spades in partner's hand.

Responder is forced to bid until game is reached, even with *no* points. Remember opener wants to be in game, or possibly slam. Responder's job is to help find the best spot. Since responder is forced to bid, it becomes necessary to have ways of showing some values and bids which show weak hands. A hand with 7 or more points in high cards or counting distribution, if you can raise partner's suit, is considered a good hand. There are two weak responses (less than 7 points) after partner has opened with two of a suit.

1. A response of 2NT is weak. It may or may not be a balanced hand. It merely shows a weak hand with little or no trump support.
2. A raise of your partner's suit to game shows a weak hand. It shows adequate trump support (Qxx,xxxx or better) with little or nothing else. If partner opened with 2♠, a raise to 3♠ is a stronger bid than a raise to 4♠. The reason for this is that with some values, it is better to leave more bidding room to be able to communicate more information in case there may be a slam.

All bids, other than 2NT or a direct raise to game, show hands with 7 or more points.

Partner opens with 2♡ and you have

1.
♠ Q 7 6 4 2
♥ 4
♦ 8 7 4
♣ 9 5 3 2

2.
♠ 10 2
♥ Q 7 4 2
♦ 4 3 2
♣ 8 4 3 2

1. Bid 2NT. A bid of 2♠ would show 7+ points. 2NT is an artificial bid saying that you have a weak hand. If partner rebids 3♡, you should bid 3♠ next. Partner now knows that you have a weak hand and a spade suit.
2. Bid 4♡. Your hand is weak. This bid says, "Partner, you wanted to be in game and I have nothing more to contribute." A bid of 3♡ would be used for hands with which you want to leave room to communicate to determine if the hands fit well so that you might be able to make slam. It would also show over 7 points.

One other strong opening bid available is a bid of 2NT. It shows 22-24 high card points and is balanced. This bid is not forcing, but if responder has as many as 3 points, game should be bid, as there are about 26 points between the two hands. In this case, there is no room to invite game, so assume partner is in the middle (23). Therefore, if as responder, you have 3 points, the partnership has 26 points and you should be in game.

Opening 3NT shows a balanced hand of 25-26-27 high card points.

North
- ♠ J 3 2
- ♥ 3
- ♦ J 5 4 3
- ♣ 7 6 5 4 2

West
- ♠ 10 4
- ♥ K 8 7 6 2
- ♦ 8 7
- ♣ K Q J 3

East
- ♠ 8 7 6
- ♥ Q J 10 5 4
- ♦ A 10 9 2
- ♣ 10

South
- ♠ A K Q 9 5
- ♥ A 9
- ♦ K Q 6
- ♣ A 9 8

THE AUCTION

North	East	South	West
pass	pass	2♠	pass
4♠	pass	pass	pass

West selects the K of clubs as the opening lead. (Without touching honors he would lead fourth best.) Declarer wins with the A. Although it's important to pull trumps early, with this hand, you need to trump a heart in dummy first. Play the ace of hearts and trump a heart, then pull trump. Notice if you play three rounds of trumps first, you will have no trumps left in dummy with which to trump your little heart. Finish the play of this hand.

1. An opening bid of 2♡ is game forcing._____ T/F
2. An opening bid of 2NT is game forcing._____ T/F
3. A 2NT response to a 2♠ opener is weak._____ T/F
4. A 4♡ response to a 2♡ opener is weak._____ T/F
5. A 2◇ opening bid shows_____or more cards in the diamond suit.
6. If you open with 2♡ you either have a lot of points, or you can count_____or more tricks in your hand.
7. For a 2◇ opener, you would need to have, at least,_____tricks in your own hand.
8. After a 2♣ opening bid, a response of 2♡ shows_____or more points.
9. After a 2♡ opening, a response of 3♡ shows_____or more points.
10. An opening bid of 2NT shows_____to_____high-card points.

What do you open with these hands:

11.	♠	A	K	10	9	5	3
	♥	2					
	◆	A	K	Q	10		
	♣	A	7				

12.	♠	2				
	♥	J	10	8	7	2
	◆	A	K	7		
	♣	A	K	Q	J	

13.	♠	A	7	6		
	♥	A	K			
	◆	K	Q	6	5	2
	♣	K	Q	J		

14.	♠	A	K			
	♥	K	Q	10	3	2
	◆	A	K	Q	3	
	♣	3	2			

An overcall is a bid of a suit or NT made after an opponent has opened the auction. Sometimes there are no problems. If you have

♠ A K 6 5 4
♥ K 6 5 4
♦ K 5
♣ 9 8

and the opponents open 1♥, you would bid 1♠, just as you would have had the opponents not opened the auction.

If, however, you were about to bid 1♦ with this hand and the person in front of

♠ A 3
♥ K 6 5 4
♦ K 9 7 4
♣ K 6 5

you bid 1♥, you have a new set of conditions.

Because of the fact that you often have new problems when the opponents bid before you, it is necessary to establish what an overcall shows. There are two basic styles of overcalls. One is to bid your long suit for nuisance value and to direct the lead. You would make this bid even if your hand were weak. The other style is that the overcall, in addition to showing a suit, shows an opening or near opening hand. In this course, we will use the "good hand" overcalls. This way partner knows you have a good hand and can respond to your overcall without having to guess at whether or not you have values.

Following this theory, the person making the overcall should have at least a five-card suit, usually a good suit, and an opening hand or a near opener, 11-12 points up to about 17 points. (There are other ways to show bigger hands.) The hand should have 10 or more high-card points. Since suit quality is important, don't overcall with a poor suit, unless your hand has extra values.

The opponents have opened 1♦ and you have

1. ♠ K J 4
   ♥ A K 10 6 5
   ♦ 7 4 3
   ♣ 5 4

2. ♠ A 3
   ♥ J 7 5 4 2
   ♦ Q 5 4
   ♣ K 6 2

3. ♠ A Q 8 6 4
   ♥ A K 9 7 5
   ♦ 6
   ♣ 8 7

4. ♠ A 6
   ♥ J 7 5 4 2
   ♦ A 6 5
   ♣ A Q 5

1. Bid 1♥. You have a near opener, 11 high card points, a doubleton, and a good heart suit.

2. Pass. Your hand is minimal and your suit is bad.

3. Bid 1♠. If partner doesn't raise spades, you intend to bid hearts next.

4. Bid 1♡. Your suit isn't good, but your hand is.

When the opponents take your bid away, you should usually pass, unless you are able to overcall 1NT. A NT overcall shows a fairly balanced hand of 15-16 up to 18 points with the opening bid suit well stopped. If the opponent has opened 1♠ and you have

1.	♠	A Q 5 4 3		2.	♠	A J 3		3.	♠	A Q 4	
	♥	K 7 6			♥	K 6 5			♥	4 2	
	♦	A 4			♦	K J 7 2			♦	K Q 4 2	
	♣	6 5 4			♣	K Q 4			♣	Q 7 6 2	

1. Pass. The opponents took your bid away.

2. Overcall 1NT.

3. Pass. One hates to pass with 13 high card points, but you have no better choice. You were going to open 1♢. Although the opponents didn't bid your suit, they deprived you of bidding it at the one-level. You should never overcall a four-card suit at the two level.

When the suit you are going to overcall is lower ranking than the opening bid, so that you are forced to bid the suit on the two level, there is a greater need for a good suit, and the hand should be a full opening hand. This hand

♠ 6 5
♥ A 10 6 5 3
♦ K 6 5
♣ K 4 3

is suitable to overcall 1♡ over a 1♣ or 1♢ opening on your right, but should be passed over a 1♠ opening.

There are times when it is reasonable to overcall on a four-card suit. If your RHO opened 1♢ and you had

♠ A K Q 2
♥ 5 3
♦ 8 6 4
♣ A J 9 2

you would feel rather justified in bidding 1♠ with this strong four-card suit. These situations occur infrequently. Responder should still assume that partner's overcall shows a five-card suit.

RESPONDING TO OVERCALLS

The general theory in responding to an overcall is that you should bid as much as you think you can make. Any time you have enough points and *three* or more card support of your partner's suit, you can raise, since partner presumably has a five-card suit. **A raise of partner's overcall from one to two shows 6-10 points, including distribution. A raise to three shows 11-12 points, and is not forcing. A raise to game shows 13 or more.** Remember distribution is escalated when raising partner's suit.

With no fit for partner's suit, you should usually pass with 6-7 points or less. If you have the opponents' suit well covered and your hand is suitable for NT, bid 1NT with 8-10 points, 2NT with 11-12 and 3NT with 13 or more. If you have three or more cards of partner's major, it is usually better to stay with the major rather than bidding NT. Bidding your own suit after partner has overcalled is not forcing but shows a good long suit.

If your opponent bid 1♡ and your partner overcalls 1♠ and you have

1. ♠ A 3
   ♡ A J 4
   ♦ K 5 4 3
   ♣ 6 5 4 2

2. ♠ A 5 4
   ♡ A 6 5
   ♦ Q 7 6 5 3
   ♣ 5 4

3. ♠ A 6 5
   ♡ 5 4 3
   ♦ K 4
   ♣ A Q 7 6 5

4. ♠ 3 2
   ♡ 7 6 4
   ♦ Q 5 4
   ♣ K Q 6 5 4

1. Bid 2NT.
2. Bid 3♠.
3. Bid 4♠, remember 2♣ isn't forcing.
4. Pass. You have only 7 points so you have no need to bid, and you have some tolerance for spades.

QUIZ

Your right hand opponent opens with 1♡ and you have

1. ♠ 9 7 5 3 2
   ♡ A 6 5
   ♦ A Q 4
   ♣ 5 4

2. ♠ A K Q 6 5
   ♡ 7 6
   ♦ Q 4 3
   ♣ 6 5 2

3. ♠ 7 6
   ♡ Q 4 3
   ♦ J 9 8 7 4
   ♣ A K J

4. ♠ A 3
   ♡ A Q 6 5 4
   ♦ K 8 7
   ♣ 8 7 5

5. ♠ J 9 8 7 4
   ♡ A 8
   ♦ A K 8 7
   ♣ K 4

Your left hand opponent opened 1♢. Your partner has overcalled 1♠ and the next player passed. You have

6. ♠ 7 6 5 3
   ♡ A 7 6
   ♦ 2
   ♣ A 8 7 5 3

7. ♠ 7 6 4
   ♡ 9 7 3 2
   ♦ A 8 7 6
   ♣ K 2

8. ♠ 5 4
   ♡ 7 5 4
   ♦ A Q 7 6
   ♣ A 8 7 4

9. ♠ 8 6 4 3
   ♡ 2
   ♦ A 8 7 6
   ♣ A K 7 6

10. ♠ 8 6
    ♡ Q 6 5
    ♦ A 7 5 3
    ♣ 8 6 4 3

11. ♠ 5 2
    ♡ A 6 3
    ♦ A Q 8 7
    ♣ A 7 6 3

12. ♠ Q 8 7 6 3
    ♥ — — —
    ♦ 9 8 7 4
    ♣ A Q 6 5

13. ♠ 4
    ♥ A K 8 6 3 2
    ♦ 9 7
    ♣ J 7 6 3

14. ♠ 7 6
    ♥ A 8 7
    ♦ K J 10
    ♣ K 8 7 6 4

15. ♠ 8 5 2
    ♥ 6 5
    ♦ 8 7 5
    ♣ A K 7 6 5

There are different ways of playing single jump overcalls, such as jumping to 2♠ or 3♣ over an opponent's 1♦ opening. In rubber bridge circles, the most common way of playing the single jump overcall is that it is stronger than an overcall, or roughly 18-21 or 22 points. It is not forcing, but urges partner to bid a game if he has anything at all. A jump to 3♥ or 3♠, however is a double jump so is totally different. The double jump shows a weak hand with a very long suit, intended as a nuisance or preemptive (see chapter XII) bid. Using this idea, after a 1♥ opening by your right hand opponent, 2♠, 3♣, and 3♦ by you would be strong, and 3♠ would be weak.

ANSWERS TO QUIZ ON OVERCALLS

1. Pass
2. 1♠
3. Pass
4. Pass—The opponents took your bid.
5. 1♥
6. 3♠
7. 2♠—You have three card support and your partner is known to have five.
8. 1 NT
9. 4♥
10. Pass
11. 3 NT
12. 4♠—Counting 5 points for the void, your hand evaluates to 13 points.
13. 2♥
14. 2 NT
15. 2♣—Avoid bidding 2♣ as that isn't forcing, and you already know that you have at least eight cards in spades.

VIII
FORCING BIDS

One of the most important considerations in bidding is to know which bids are forcing and which bids can be passed. A forcing bid is one which partner cannot pass at the next turn. Some bids are forcing all the way to game and some are forcing only for one round. Since there are so many possible auctions, a few generalizations are necessary. We learned in Chapter V that when we know where a contract should be played and that there are enough points for game, at our second bid we should bid the game, either as opener or responder. Forcing bids are needed when we don't know as yet where a contract should be played.

THE MOST COMMON FORCING BID BY OPENER IS A JUMP SHIFT (1♡— 1♠—3♣). Since this shows 19+ points, it is *game* forcing because with the 6 points guaranteed by responder, there are enough points for game. If you open this hand with 1♡ and partner responds 1♠, you need to rebid 3♣, as partner could pass 2♣.

♠ A 4
♥ K Q J 7 4
♦ 5 3
♣ A K J 2

You want to be in game with this hand even if partner has only 6-7 points, but at this point you don't know where.

Opener's rebid of a new suit is not forcing (1♡—1♠—2♣). It doesn't even guarantee extra values. This would show a hand of five or more hearts, and four or more clubs, and from 13-18 points. Notice that it may be more than a minimum, but denies as many as 19.

Opener's rebid of a jump to 2NT is also game forcing (1♦—1♡—2NT). This shows a balanced hand that was too big to open 1NT. It has 19, 20 or 21 points. If you hold

♠ A .K J
♥ K 3 2
♦ A J 5 4 3
♣ K 2

and the auction has gone 1♦—1♡, jump to 2NT. If partner rebids 3♡, you would raise to 4♡, as partner's rebidding them would guarantee five or more hearts. If partner bids 3♣ over your 2NT, you should bid 3♡ next. This will show a three-card heart suit. If you had four of them, you would have raised immediately over 1♡. Partner will not pass anything short of game, as your 2NT rebid was game forcing.

If opener jumps in his own suit or in partner's, it shows extra values, (17-18 points), but it is not forcing. Responder could pass with only 6-7, but should bid with more than 7. If the bidding had gone 1♣ by you, as opener, and you held

♠ A Q 4 3
♥ 2
♦ A 4 2
♣ K Q 5 4 3

if partner responded 1♠, you would rebid 3♠. This would say that you have a very nice hand, about 17 (good 16, 17-18), and have a definite interest in game, but you can't do it by yourself. Note that if you had any more points, say another Q, which would give you 20 points, you would bid game directly. One other point on this hand: to rebid your club suit would be unthinkable. It's much more important to let your partner know you have found a major suit to have as trump than to tell about your five-card club suit.

Suppose you open 1♦ with the following hand

♠ A 7 6 5
♥ 9
♦ A K Q 6 4
♣ K Q 2

After you open with 1♦, your partner responds 1♠. What is your rebid as opener? Now that you have found a trump suit, you count everything (HCP and distribution). Bid a direct 4♠. This bid shows 19-20-21 points. Remember, any jump by opener shows a strong hand.

Suppose there is a slam! The responder knows that opener has about 20 points. If responder has a hand such as:

♠ K Q 3 2
♥ K 8 7
♦ 3 2
♣ A 9 8 2

It is responder who knows that slam is likely. He should bid 4NT and if opener shows 2 or 3 Aces, responder should bid 6♠.

RESPONDER HAS MANY FORCING BIDS. We have already learned that immediate jumps are forcing. (1♥—3♥) or 1♥—2NT) and, of course, a jump shift (1♦—2♠) is forcing. These are all game forcing bids, as they announce opening hands or better.

After partner's opening bid of one of a suit, a new suit by responder is forcing (1♦—1♠), as the point range for this bid is 6-18 points. **A two-over-one bid (1♥ - 2♦) is, of course, forcing as it shows at least 10-18 points.** Since a new suit bid by responder can be on as few as 6 points (on the one level) or could be big, it is forcing for one round. Responder will usually jump shift with as many as 19 points, but doesn't have to if, for example, he doesn't have a five card suit. Occasionally, therefore, the new suit bid by responder will actually be more than 18 points.

Responder's new suit bids below the game level are forcing even at later turns if NT has not been bid. In the auction (1♣—1♦—1♥—1♠), 1♠ is forcing or (1♣—1♥— 2♣—2♦), 2♦ is forcing. For the latter auction, your hand might be

♠ 4 2
♥ A K 9 7 6
♦ A K 5 3
♣ 9 8

You know you want to be in game, as you have an opener opposite an opener, but you are not in a position to decide where. This is the reason that new suits by responder need to be forcing.

If NT *has* been bid, such as, (1♦—1♠—1NT—2♣), 2♣ is not forcing. You would have to jump to 3♣ to force. This is to allow you to play in a suit at a low level if your hand is weak. Partner's 1NT rebid shows a balanced hand with 12, 13, or 14 high card points. If you hold the following

♠ A 7 6 5 2
♥ 4
♦ 4 3
♣ K 9 7 3 2

you would like to have either spades or clubs as trump rather than play in NT, but you don't want to be very high as your hand is weak. Partner could pass your 2♣ bid or could bid 2♠ if he likes spades better than clubs.

If an auction proceeds (1♥—1NT—2♣—2♦), 2♦ is not forcing, because the original 1NT limited the hand to 6-10 high card points. This is a hand that you would have bid 2♦ at your first response, but your hand wasn't good enough for a two-over-one bid, such as

♠ 6 5 4
♥ 4
♦ A Q 5 4 3 2
♣ 6 4 2

If responder, at his second turn, jumps in opener's suit, it is not forcing (1♦—1♥—1♠—3♠) because when responder knows where the contract is going to be played (spades) if he has enough points for game, at his second bid, he should bid the game himself. In the above auction, the 3♠ bid shows nearly an opening hand, such as

♠ A 4 3 2
♥ K 8 7 4
♦ 5 4
♣ K 3 2

You want to be in game, unless partner is on a very minimum opener.

Responder's jump in his own suit, however, shows an opening hand with a long suit and is forcing. If you held this hand over partner's 1♦ opening, you would bid 1♥

♠ A 3
♥ A K 7 6 5 3
♦ Q 5
♣ 7 6 5

and if partner rebid 2♦, you should jump to 3♥. You know that you want to be in game, but you are not in a position to bid it as you don't know, as yet, where it should be played.

There are certain conditions in which bids have a different meaning. Once you have passed you are known to have less than 13 points, so most previously forcing bids are no longer forcing. Examine the following auctions:

North	East	South	West
pass	pass	1♠	pass
3♠			

or

North	East	South	West
pass	pass	1♥	pass
2NT			

North's bid of 3♠ shows a near opener, 11-12 points, with spade support. 2NT shows a balanced 11-12 high cards without adequate trump support. When partner opens after you have previously passed, if you have a hand with which you want to be in game because your hand fits well, you must bid game directly. If you held this hand

♠ A 5 4 2
♥ 3
♦ K Q J 2
♣ 8 7 4 2

and the bidding has gone pass by you, pass by your LHO, partner opens 1♠, pass by RHO, the only way of insuring getting to game is by bidding 4♠. Even a new suit bid by you would not be forcing.

If your side has a part score, there are added inferences drawn if partner bids beyond what you need to make a game. Suppose you have a 40 part score and have the following auction: you open 1♥ and partner bids 3♥. His 3♥ bid would normally be forcing, but you will complete your game by making 3♥, so now it isn't forcing. However, 2♥ would have been enough for game, so why did partner bid 3♥? He must be suggesting a slam. If your hand is a minimum, you should pass, but if you have extra values, you might investigate a slam.

A RECOMMENDATION which prevents many bidding problems—When partner has opened and you change suits on the two level, such as 1♠—2♣, if partner limits his hand by rebidding 2NT you can pass. If he changes suits or rebids his suit, you promise another bid. For example, 1♠—2♣—2♠, you are expected to bid again.

An Advanced Bidding Point: One other forcing bid by opener, which is standard among very experienced bridge players, is a reverse (1♦—1♠—2♥). The second suit bid by opener is higher ranking than the first suit and it is on the two level. This bid takes up a lot of bidding room. If partner should happen to be short in hearts but has some diamonds, he would have to bid on the three level to return to your first bid suit. For you to be willing for the auction to get that high, you should have a big hand, such as

♠ A 6
♥ A K J 3
♦ A J 10 7 3
♣ 7 5

Recap for Common Forcing Bids if you are below the game level

FORCING 1ST BIDS BY RESPONDER
New Suit Bid
Jump in Partner's Suit
Jump Shift
Jump to 2NT

FORCING REBIDS BY OPENER
Jump Shift
Jump to 2NT
A Reverse

FORCING 2ND BIDS BY RESPONDER
Jump in Your Own Suit
New Suit (If 1NT has been bid, a new suit
wouldn't be forcing. If opener
rebid 1NT, a jump would be needed).

When the opponents interfere in your auction, there is the additional forcing bid available of cue bidding the opponents' suit. This shows a big hand and is forcing to game.

Also, new suits are forcing when a previously bid suit has been supported, such as 1♡—2♡—3♣.

QUIZ ON FORCING BIDS

Which of the underlined bids are forcing:

	Opener	Reponder		Opener	Reponder
1.	1♥	<u>1NT</u>	12.	1♥	1♠
2.	1♠	<u>2NT</u>		<u>3♣</u>	
3.	1♦	<u>1♥</u>	13.	1♦	1♠
4.	1♠	<u>2♣</u>		2♦	<u>2♠</u>
5.	1♦	<u>2♠</u>	14.	1♣	1♥
6.	1♦	<u>3NT</u>		2♣	<u>3♣</u>
7.	1♥	1♠	15.	1♥	1♠
	<u>2♠</u>			2♥	<u>2NT</u>
8.	1♥	1♠	16.	1♥	1♠
	<u>3♠</u>			2♥	<u>3♣</u>
9.	1♣	1♥	17.	1♥	1NT
	<u>2NT</u>			2♣	<u>2♦</u>
10.	1♦	1♥	18.	1♦	1♠
	<u>3♦</u>			2♦	<u>3♠</u>
11.	1♣	1♠			
	<u>4♠</u>				

Answers:
2, 3, 4, 5, 9, 12, 16, 18.

IX

TAKE-OUT DOUBLES

A bid of "double" has more than one meaning in bridge. It is most often used for the purpose of increasing the points you receive if the opponents fail to make a contract. If the opponents bid 4♠ and you think you can defeat the contract, you would double. If you are right, you would reap the rewards.

There is another common meaning of the double. A *take-out* double is used as a request for partner to bid. If your right hand opponent opened with 1◇ and you have

♠ A 8 6 4
♥ K J 7 6
♦ 4
♣ A J 6 5

you would like to be able to bid with your 13 + 2 points, but you have no five-card suit to overcall. Actually you have three fairly good suits. You should double with this hand, which tells partner to pick one of the three unbid suits. Whichever he picks will be okay with you.

It is always a pleasant experience to know what partner's bids mean and for partner to have some idea as to the meaning of your bids. A double which is intended for "take-out" as opposed to penalty is used in specific situations.

A take-out double is made at your first opportunity to double the suit bid, partner has either passed or not had an opportunity to bid, and it must be below the game level. It shows an opening hand or better and the hand should contain three or more cards of the unbid suits, as partner is asked to pick one of "your" suits. (An exception can be made to the distributional requirement if the hand has substantial extra values.)

Examine the following auctions to determine which of the following doubles are take-out and which are penalty.

	North	East	South	West
1.	1♥	Dbl		
2.	1♥	pass	1NT	pass
	2♥	Dbl		
3.	1♠	2♦	Dbl	
4.	1NT	pass	4♠	Dbl
5.	1♥	pass	1♠	Dbl

1. Take-out.
2. Penalty. - It was not the first opportunity to double this suit.
3. Penalty. - Partner has made a bid.
4. Penalty. - The opponents are at the game level.
5. Take-out. - Partner has not bid and it is your first opportunity to double. Since the opponents have bid two suits, your double shows the remaining two suits.

Consider the following hands after your right hand opponent opens with 1 ◇.

1. ♠ A 6 5 4
    ♥ A J 5
    ♦ 7 6
    ♣ K J 7 6

2. ♠ A
    ♥ K 4 3 2
    ♦ 8 7 6 5
    ♣ A Q 7 6

3. ♠ A 8 7 6
    ♥ A 8 7 6
    ♦ 4
    ♣ K 8 7 6

4. ♠ A J 8 7 6
    ♥ Q 6 5
    ♦ 6 5
    ♣ A Q 5

1. This is a good take-out double. If partner bids any of the other three suits, you have support.
2. Pass. You don't have spades. You need to have support for any suit partner might bid, unless you have a very big hand.
3. Double. This is a minimum for a take-out double, but it qualifies.
4. Bid 1♠. This qualifies for a double, but with a good five card suit, it is better to bid your suit, especially when it is a major suit.

When partner has made a take-out double, unless your right hand opponent bids, you are basically forced to bid. If you don't, you will turn your partner's take-out double into penalty by your pass. If partner has made a take-out double of 1♡ with this hand

♠ A 6 5 4   and you have   ♠ 8 7 3 2
♥ 5   ♥ 8 7 4 3
♦ A 6 5 4   ♦ J 3 2
♣ A 6 5 4   ♣ K 3

it seems that one would like to pass, but consider the consequences. If you pass, your side will presumably take four tricks. This means the opponents will make their contract-1♡ doubled = 60, plus 50 for the insult, plus 100 or 200 for each overtrick that they make, depending on vulnerability. You would lose from 300 to 500 points. If you bid your long suit, as requested, you may not make it, but the penalty would be small.

When partner has made a take-out double and the next person passes, the only time you pass is when you want to defend. You have five or more very good cards in the opponents' suit and a fairly good hand. If partner makes a take-out double of 1♠, you could pass with

♠ A K J 10 8
♥ A 6 5
♦ 7 6 5
♣ 6 5

You are happy to defend 1♠ doubled. If the opponents try to escape to a new suit, partner will be able to double that.

UNLESS YOU HAVE A HAND WHICH YOU ARE WILLING TO DEFEND, BECAUSE YOU EXPECT TO SET THE OPPONENTS, YOU MUST BID OVER

Since you are basically forced to bid, it is important to distinguish between hands with which you are glad to bid and hands that you are bidding only because you must. If partner makes a takeout double, consider these two hands.

1. ♠ 5 4 3 2   2. ♠ Q 7 6 5 4
   ♥ 6 4   ♥ 4 3 2
   ♦ K J 6   ♦ A K 2
   ♣ 5 4 3 2   ♣ 3 2

If you bid 1♠ with each of these hands, partner would not know when to bid again. **Since you were forced to bid, you need to distinguish between bad hands and good hands.** Therefore, responding to a take-out double must be different than responding to partner's opening bid. **A bid of a suit at the cheapest level shows 0-8 points, a one-level jump equals 9-11 points, and hands of about opening strength are bid directly to game.** You would bid 1♠ with hand 1 above, and bid 2♠ with hand 2.

Since the doubler's hand tends to be short in the suit bid, he prefers to hear partner bid a suit, rather than no trump. Nevertheless, you may have some hands where no trump seems like the best spot. Since partner's hand is more oriented towards suit play when he makes the take-out double, your no trump responses should be made on fairly good hands. **In response to a take-out double, with 8-10 high card points and the opponents' suit well stopped, bid 1NT. With 11-12 HCP and the opponents' suit well stopped, bid 2NT. With 13 or more points and the opponents' suit well stopped, bid 3NT.** If you have four or more cards in a major, bid that suit in preference to no trump.

A double of 1NT has a different meaning than a double of a suit bid. It shows a hand as good as or better than the opening NT bid. Partner should pass the double if it appears that his side has more than half of the points and therefore expects to defeat the contract.

REBIDDING AFTER MAKING A TAKE-OUT DOUBLE

When the bidding comes back to you after you have made a take-out double, you will know the approximate size of partner's hand. If he had an opening hand, be would go directly to game. If not, he would bid something less than game and you would have to decide if game is a possibility.

If you have made a take-out double of 1♡ with
♠ A 4 3 2
♥ 3 2
♦ K J 3 2
♣ A J 2

and partner responded 1♠, you should pass at your next turn. Partner has at best 8 points and you have 14. There are no more than 22 points between the two hands. Game is out of the question, since 26 points are needed, so there is no point in taking another bid. Notice that this is a totally different situation than when you have opened the bidding and partner has responded with one of a suit.

If you made a take-out double of 1♠ with

♠ 3
♥ A 9 8 7
♦ A 8 7 6
♣ K Q 4 3

and partner responded with 2♡, pass. Partner didn't jump. This was the minimum level that partner could bid his heart suit. Partner's bid shows 0-8 points.

If you made a take-out double of 1♡ with

♠ A 5 4 3
♥ 3 2
♦ A 8 3 2
♣ A K J

and partner responded with 2♠, showing 9-11 points, bid 4♠. You have 17 points. Even if partner has only 9 points, there are enough for game.

If you made a take-out double of 1◇ with

♠ A 4 3 2
♥ A Q 4 2
♦ 3 2
♣ A 3 2

and partner bids 2♠, there may be a game. You have 15 points. If partner has 9, you are short, but if partner has 11, there are enough. Bid 3♠. This invites partner to go on. With 9 points, he should pass; with 11, he should bid game, and with 10 he must make a judgment decision.

WHEN REBIDDING AFTER MAKING A TAKE-OUT DOUBLE, ADD YOUR POINTS TO WHAT PARTNER HAS ANNOUNCED AND IF THERE ARE ENOUGH POINTS FOR GAME, BID IT. IF THERE ARE NOT ENOUGH POINTS FOR GAME, PASS. IF THERE ARE POSSIBLY ENOUGH POINTS, MAKE AN INVITATIONAL BID. Anytime you make a take-out double and bid again, you show extra values.

An Advanced Point - If partner bids the opponents' suit after a take-out double, it is not because of wanting to play it there. If partner has good cards in the opponents' suit, he would either pass for penalty or bid NT. Therefore, a bid of the opponents' suit after a take-out double has special meaning. It says that there are enough points for game, but there is a problem in deciding what would be the best game. If partner "cue" bids the opponents' suit, you should cooperate in the search for the best game by bidding your best suit.

QUIZ ON TAKE-OUT DOUBLES

Indicate whether the double is for take-out or penalty in the following auctions.

	North	East	South	West
1.	1♠	2♥	Dbl	
2.	1♠	pass	2♠	Dbl
3.	1NT	2♥	Dbl	

4.	1♠	pass	2♣	Dbl
5.	2♠	pass	4♠	Dbl
6.	1♠	pass	pass	Dbl

If your right hand opponent opens 1♡, what do you do with the following hands?

7.	♠ A K 4 3 2	8.	♠ A	9.	♠ K 8 6 2
	♥ 4 3		♥ K 4 3 2		♥ 4 3
	♦ A 3 2		♦ Q 6 4 2		♦ A K 4 2
	♣ Q 6 4		♣ K 7 6 2		♣ Q J 2

10.	♠ A J	11.	♠ 8 4 3 2
	♥ K J 4		♥ 4
	♦ A Q 2		♦ A K 4 3 2
	♣ J 6 4 3 2		♣ A J 3

12. Your RHO opened 1♡, you made a take-out double and partner responded 1♠. What is your next call with this hand?

♠ A 4 3 2
♥ 4 3
♦ A J 9
♣ K 6 5 2

13. With the same conditions, what do you do if partner responded 2♠?

14. Your RHO opened 1♡, you made a take-out double and partner responded with 2♣. What is your next call?

♠ A J 3 2
♥ 4 2
♦ A K 4 2
♣ 9 4 2

15. Your RHO opened 1♦, you doubled and partner bid 2♠. What is your next call with this hand?

♠ A Q 4 2
♥ K 4 3 2
♦ 4 2
♣ A J 4

Answers to quiz on take-out doubles

1. Penalty	9. Double
2. Take-out	10. 1NT
3. Penalty	11. Double
4. Take-out	12. Pass
5. Penalty	13. Pass
6. Take-out	14. Pass. Another bid would show extra values.
7. Bid 1♥	15. Bid 3♠. This invites partner to bid 4 if he is at the top of his bid.
8. Pass	

X

NO TRUMP AND THE STAYMAN CONVENTION

26 points = game
33 points = small slam
37 points = grand slam

Review of 1NT opening—A 1 NT opening bid shows a hand of 15, 16, 17 or 18 high card points and is rather balanced, meaning no singletons or voids, and no more than one doubleton. Distribution is never counted when bidding NT.

After your partner has opened 1NT and you, as responder, are pleased to play in NT, you bid as follows:

0-7   Usually pass. Some exceptions will be shown later.

8-9   The partnership may or may not have the 26 points needed for game in NT. Bid 2NT. This invites the opener to go to game (3NT) if he is in the upper part of his range, 17-18 points.

10-14   Bid 3NT. You want to be in game, no more, no less.

15-16   There is at least a game, possibly a slam. Bid 4NT. Partner will notice that you bid one beyond game. Since it is pointless to be in 4NT when 3NT is game, this asks partner to bid 6NT if he is on top of his bid, 17 or 18, but to pass with 15 or 16.

17-18   Bid 6NT. Your combined points are 32-36. When you are at worst within one point of what you need, bid it.

19-20   You have at least a small slam, possibly a grand. Bid 5NT. This forces at least 6NT and invites a grand slam. If partner is on 15 or 16 he bids 6NT, but with 17 or 18 he bids 7NT.

If partner opens 1NT and you have the following hands, plan your responses.

1.	♠	4 3 2	2.	♠	A J 2	3.	♠	A 4
	♥	A 4		♥	3 2		♥	4 3 2
	♦	8 7 5 2		♦	K Q J 4		♦	8 6 5 2
	♣	Q 6 5 2		♣	7 5 3 2		♣	A 5 4 2

4.	♠	A 4 3	5.	♠	5 3 2
	♥	A K J		♥	A K 2
	♦	3 2		♦	K Q 3 2
	♣	K Q J 3 2		♣	K J 4

1. Pass. You have only 6 points, so the partnership has, at best, 24 points (6 + 18) which is not enough for game, so there is no point in bidding. Notice that when partner opens with one of a suit, you should bid with 6 points as partner could be on as many as 20 + points and you could miss a game. A 1NT opening has a maximum of 18 points.

2. Bid 3NT as you are the one who knows that the points are sufficient for game. It should not be of concern to you that you have honors in only two suits. Partner's hand is better than yours, so he rates to have cards in the other suits. You have enough points for game and NT seems like the best bet.

3. This is a situation in which you can't be sure of game, as you have 8 points. If partner has only 15 or 16, you would not want to be in game, but if partner has 17 or 18, you would have a combined 25 or 26 and game would likely make. Bid 2NT. This says "we could have game, partner." Opener should pass with 15 or 16, but accept the invitation with 17 or 18.

4. Bid a direct 6NT. This may be a traumatic experience the first time you do it, but the points are there for a small slam. So bid it!

5. You have 16 points, which is clearly enough for game and could be enough for slam. If opener has 15 or 16, game would be high enough, but if opener has 17 or 18, you would want to be in slam. Bid 4NT, one more than necessary for game. This invites partner to go to slam. He will pass with 15 or 16, but bid 6NT with 17 or 18.

Sometimes, as responder, you have a weak hand, with no interest in game, but you would rather play in a suit than in NT. If, for example, you hold

♠ 7 6 5
♥ J 8 7 6 3 2   This bid is known affectionately as the "drop dead" bid.
♦ 3 2
♣ 3 2

and partner opens 1NT, you can easily see that your hand rates to take no tricks if you pass. Also, your combined point count is 16-19, less than half the deck. Since your hand probably has no entries, your partner would have to play entirely out of his hand, which is a great disadvantage. You would like, therefore, to be able to bid 2♥, and have partner pass, as your hand will take some tricks with hearts as trump. For this reason, bids of 2♦, 2♥ and 2♠, over a 1NT opening, are weak bids, 0-7 HCP with at least five cards of the suit bid. (A bid of 2♣ will be discussed later, as it is a special bid) It is rare in bridge to take a bid with a very weak hand. In these situations it is done to improve the contract. Opener should, in general, pass the response of 2♦, ♥ or ♠. The only time he should bid again after he has opened 1NT and you have bid 2♥, for example, is when he has a maximum hand and has a heart fit.

As an example, if you opened 1NT with

♠ K 9 7
♥ K J 10
♦ A K 9 8 7
♣ A 7

and partner bids 2♥. Even though partner has shown a weak hand, you really like his heart bid. Bid 3♥, which says "Unless your hand is really sick, bid 4H." He should pass with a hand such as

♠ 4 3   but should raise to 4♥ with   ♠ 2
♥ Q 6 4 3 2   ♥ Q 7 6 4 3 2
♦ 6 4 2   ♦ 5 3
♣ 8 6 3   ♣ K 5 4 3.

Many game-going hands with a long minor suit are better off played in NT, since it is often easier to take nine tricks in NT than 11 tricks in clubs or diamonds. If partner opens 1NT and you have

♠ Q J
♥ 6 5 4
♦ A K 4 3 2
♣ 4 3 2

bid 3NT as that will make more often than 5 ♦ even if partner has good diamonds.

However, if it can be determined that the partnership owns eight or more cards of a major suit, that is usually a safer contract. If you have

♠ 4 3
♥ A J 6 4 3
♦ A J 5
♣ 6 4 3

and partner opens 1NT, you know you have enough points for game. If partner has three or more hearts, you would want to be in 4 ♥, but if partner has a doubleton heart, you would want to be in 3NT. You can't bid 2 ♥ as that is a weak bid. Bid 3 ♥, which says that you want to be at least in game and that you have a five-card heart suit. Partner should raise to 4 ♥ with three or more hearts, and bid 3NT with a doubleton.

If partner opens 1NT and you have

♠ A J 8 6 5 3
♥ K 6 4
♦ 6 5
♣ 4 3

bid 4 ♠. You know there are at least eight spades between the hands, as partner can have no singletons. Also, you can count your distribution when you know you are going to play in a suit.

Many times, when responding to an opening bid of 1NT, you will have hands with one or more four-card major suits. These are the hands that are difficult to handle. This is why the **Stayman Convention** has become so popular. A "convention" is a bid which shows nothing about the suit bid, but rather asks a question of partner or describes a particular type of hand. If partner opens 1NT and you have

♠ A 4 3 2
♥ A Q 3 2
♦ 8 7 4 3
♣ 4

you need to know specifically if partner has either four hearts or four spades. If he does, the major suit would likely be the best contract; if he does not, 3NT would be the spot.

A response of 2 ♣ over a 1NT opening is the Stayman Convention. This bid says nothing about clubs, but asks a question of the opener. It asks the opener to name a four-card major if he has one. If opener has a four-card heart suit or a four-card spade suit, he would bid it. With four of each suit, spades are shown first. If opener doesn't have a four-card major, he bids 2 ♦. This says nothing about diamonds, but rather says only that the hand does not have four hearts or four spades. If, in the above example, you bid 2 ♣ and opener rebids 2 ♦, you should bid 3NT. Opener doesn't have four hearts or four spades, so you can forget about playing in a major suit, as there is no eight-card fit. Also, you can now feel better about the club suit, since partner hasn't many cards in the majors, he is more likely to have the club suit well covered.

The Stayman Convention, used only over NT openers, is primarily used to try to locate 4-4 major suit fits. In general, it shows at least one four-card major and at least eight points. A couple of unusual uses of Stayman will be mentioned later, but normally you don't use Stayman unless you have at least one four-card major suit and eight or more high-card points.

If partner opens 1NT and you have

♠ Q 6 4 3
♥ 3 2
♦ 4 3 2
♣ A K Q 6

you begin with 2♣. If partner responds 2◇, showing no four-card major, you bid 3NT, as you have enough points for game.

If partner opened 1NT and you had

♠ 8
♥ K 6 4 3
♦ A J 3 2
♣ 8 7 5 2

you would bid 2♣. If partner now bids 2♡, you happily bid 4♡. You have enough for game, since you can count your distribution when you know you are going to be in a trump suit. If partner bids 2◇, showing no four-card major, you next bid 2NT. This shows 8-9 points, just like a direct 1NT—2NT bid, only you stopped first to ask about a major suit. Partner would pass with 15-16 HCP and bid 3NT with 17-18. If partner should bid 2♠ over your 2♣ bid, still rebid 2NT, as partner knows you were interested in a major suit. When you refuse spades, it had to have been hearts that you wanted to hear.

If partner opens 1NT, you would also use Stayman with this hand

♠ A 5 4 3
♥ A 7 6 4 2
♦ Q 4 3
♣ 3

Although you have a five-card suit, you don't want to bid 3♡, because if partner bids 3NT, you would then have no way to know if he had four spades in his hand. Start this hand with 2♣. If partner bids 2♡ or 2♠, you will raise either to game. If partner bids 2◇, you jump to 3♡, which is forcing just as a direct jump to 3♡ would be. Partner will raise to 4♡ with three hearts and bid 3NT with a doubleton heart. You now have checked out both majors before deciding where to play this hand.

If, as opener, you bid 1NT with

♠ A K 4 2
♥ A 5 4 2
♦ A 3 2
♣ Q 2

and partner bids 2♣, you would bid 2♠. If partner now bids 3NT, you should bid 4♡. Partner has expressed an interest in playing this hand in a major suit. If he wasn't interested in spades, it must be hearts.

The following are more unusual uses of Stayman. Be sure the above information is understood thoroughly before reading on.

Although Stayman is primarily used to locate 4-4 fits and with 8 or more points, there are some exceptions. Suppose your partner opens 1NT and you have

♠ J 7 6 4
♥ 7 6 5 3
♦ 8 7 6 4 2
♣ — — —

You could improve your chances of a plus score if you could play this in one of your suits. Bid 2♣. Partner will, of course, think you have 8 + points, but that's okay. He will soon find out what you are doing, because when he rebids 2◇, 2♡ or 2♠, you pass. Remember when responding to Stayman, those are his only choices. He either has a four-card major and bids it, or says he doesn't have one by bidding 2◇.

If partner opens 1NT and you have   ♠ A 10 4 3 2
                                       ♥ K 3 2
                                       ♦ J 3 2
                                       ♣ 4 2

your hand is too good to respond 2♠ (0-7 HCP) and not good enough for 3♠ (10 + HCP) This is one of the few exceptions when you use Stayman with a five-card major suit. You bid 2♣. If partner bids 2♠, you raise to 4♠, but if partner bids 2◇ or 2♡, you bid 2♠. This shows exactly five spades and 8-9 high card points.

If your partner opens 1NT and you have a bad hand with long clubs, it is usually best to pass. Sometimes you can't bear to pass, because you have 0-2 points and six clubs such as:

♠ J 2
♥ 4 3
♦ 6 5
♣ 10 9 8 5 4 3

Bid 2♣ and over partner's bid of 2◇, 2♡ or 2♠, you bid 3♣. This says, "Partner, I was kidding about Stayman. I really want to play in clubs, because I have a bad hand with a long club suit."

IF PARTNER WERE TO OPEN 2NT, 3♣ IS STAYMAN. SINCE PARTNER'S HAND IS SO BIG, ONLY 3 POINTS ARE NEEDED FOR GAME; THEREFORE THIS IS ALSO ENOUGH TO USE STAYMAN.

Your partner has opened 1NT. What is your first response with the following hands?

1. ♠ K 9 7 5 3 2
   ♥ 9 7 5
   ♦ 3 2
   ♣ 6 5

2. ♠ K 9 8 6
   ♥ 4
   ♦ K 5 4 2
   ♣ 10 9 5 4

3. ♠ A J 9 8 4
   ♥ 4 3
   ♦ Q J 9 2
   ♣ K 8

4. ♠ 7 4
   ♥ Q J 10 7 6 5
   ♦ 3
   ♣ K J 4 2

5. ♠ A Q 9 7 5
   ♥ K J 6 4 2
   ♦ 9 3
   ♣ 5

6. ♠ 9 2
   ♥ Q 8 5
   ♦ K Q 5 4 3
   ♣ K 9 3

7. ♠ Q 9 7 6
   ♥ 3
   ♦ A K 6 4
   ♣ 8 7 4 2

8. ♠ 8 7
   ♥ A K 10 5 3
   ♦ K Q 4
   ♣ 10 8 4

9. ♠ A 3
   ♥ K 4 2
   ♦ K Q 9 7 5
   ♣ K 7 5

10. ♠ 9 5
    ♥ K J 8 7 6 5
    ♦ A 4 2
    ♣ 10 2

11. ♠ A Q 7 5
    ♥ A J 10 8
    ♦ 4
    ♣ A 4 3 2

12. ♠ A 10 8 6
    ♥ Q 7 6 5 4
    ♦ A 9 7 6
    ♣ — — —

Answers to quiz on No Trump and the Stayman Convention:

1. 2♥
2. Pass
3. 3♠
4. 4♥
5. 3♥—if partner bids 3NT, your next bid will be 4♥.
6. 3 NT
7. 2♣
8. 3♥
9. 4 NT
10. 4♥
11. 2♣
12. 2♣—if partner bids 2♦, you next bid 3♥.

46 ♤ *No Trump and the Stayman Convention*

XI

SLAM BIDDING

The two most important aspects of slam bidding are:
1. Knowing that there are enough points for slam (or tricks with distributional hands where tricks can be counted).
2. Knowing that the opponents can't take the first two tricks.

The person who should pursue a slam is the person who knows that the points are there. This may or may not be the person with the bigger hand. (33 points will usually yield a small slam and 37 points a grand slam.)

Partner opens 1 ◇ and you have
♠ K Q 10 2
♥ A 5 4 3 2
♦ K 3 2
♣ 6

you bid 1♡ and partner next cries 2♠. Partner has made a jump shift showing 19+ points. You know that you have a place to play (spades) and that the partnership has enough points for slam, as you have 12 high plus a singleton, which is worth 3 points when you have found a trump fit. It is up to you to pursue the slam.

You hold
♠ A 5 3
♥ A Q J 7 5
♦ A Q 5 4
♣ 7

and open 1♡. Partner bids 3♡ (13-16 points). Your hand has 17 high plus three for the singleton. The partnership has 33+ points. It is up to you to take action.

If partner opens 2NT (22-24 balanced) and you have
♠ A 4 3 2
♥ K J 4
♦ Q J 5 4
♣ 4 3

you are the one who knows that there are 33+ points. Bid 6NT.

There are many auctions in which you will know the slam is a possibility. Some of these hands contain problems. In suit bidding, there are more than 40 points in the deck as distributional points are added. It is possible to have enough points for slam, but be missing controls. The opponents could have two aces. For this reason, the Blackwood Convention has become a standard way of asking for aces. When a partnership has been bidding suits and one or the other bids 4NT, as in the auction 1♠—3♠—4NT, it asks how many aces partner has. Partner answers alphabetically.

5♣ = 0 aces (or all 4)
5♦ = 1 ace
5♥ = 2 aces
5♠ = 3 aces

If you have asked for aces and have found that you have all of them, you can check for kings by bidding 5NT. You would take this action only if you think you might be able to make a grand slam. Your partner will answer in the same pattern.

$$6\clubsuit = 0 \text{ kings (or all 4)}$$
$$6\diamondsuit = 1 \text{ king}$$
$$6\heartsuit = 2 \text{ kings}$$
$$6\spadesuit = 3 \text{ kings}$$

If you open 1♠ with

♠ A K 6 5 4
♥ K Q J 6
♦ K J 3
♣ 7

and partner bids 3♠ (13-16 points). You have 17 high plus 3 in distribution. There are sufficient points for slam, but you need to be sure partner has at least two aces. Bid 4NT. If partner replies 5♦, return to 5♠ as you are missing two aces. But if partner bids 5♡ or 5♠, bid 6♠.

Blackwood is a useful convention when properly applied. First, it should be clear that the points (or tricks) are sufficient for slam and second, you need some assurance that the opponents cannot take the first two tricks. Blackwood does not apply directly over an opening bid of 1NT or 2NT, because slams in NT are made on high card strength. The opponents can't have two aces if you have 33 high card points.

If you use Blackwood and the information you receive is not useful to you, the convention should not have been used. Suppose you open 1♠ with

♠ A Q J 5 4
♥ 5 4
♦ K 2
♣ A K J 2

and partner bids 3♠. The points are there for slam (20 + 13). If you bid 4NT and partner has one ace, you don't know what to do. If you knew that it was the ace of hearts, you would be assured that the opponents couldn't take the first two tricks. If, however, partner's ace was in diamonds, the opponents might be able to cash the first two heart tricks before you ever won the lead. For this reason cue bidding is very effective when you need to know *which* ace or aces partner has.

Cue bidding is somewhat advanced so it works best in a regular partnership. It works like this. Once a suit has been bid and raised, that suit is going to be trump. When the suit is "set" and the hands have been shown to be good enough to be at least in game, new suit bids are cue bids, showing an ace. A bidding that goes 1♠—3♠ has set spaces as the trump suit and the hand is forced to game. There would be no point in bidding a new suit at this point unless it was a cue bid, since we already have a trump suit and we can't use two trump suits. With the above hand, after partner bids 3♠, bid 4♣, which says that you have the ace of clubs. With more than one ace to cue bid, you show the cheapest one first. For example, if you have both the ace of clubs and the ace of diamonds, you would show the club ace first. If partner cue bids the ace of hearts by bidding 4♡, you should bid 6♠. If partner cue bids the ace of diamonds by bidding 4♦, return to 4♠, as you are worried about hearts. If partner also has the ace of hearts, he will bid that next.

<table>
<tr><td colspan="2" align="center">North</td><td colspan="2" align="center">You-South</td></tr>
</table>

North

♠ K Q 2
♥ J 10 8 7
♦ K Q 3
♣ A 8 7

You-South

♠ A 4 3
♥ A K Q 5 4
♦ 5 4
♣ K Q 2

Another example. You open the South hand with 1♡ and partner raises to 3♡. Your hand is worth 19 points, which means the partnership has a minimum of 32 points. That is close enough to try for a slam, but Blackwood may not give you the information you need. If partner has only one ace, you might be off two diamond tricks. An accurate way to bid these hands would be

	South	North	
	1♥	3♥	
(1)	3♠	4♣	(2)
(3)	4♥	6♥	(4)

(1)   A cue bid of the ace of spades

(2)   A cue bid of the ace of clubs

(3)   A return to the agreed upon trump suit, denying the ace of diamonds. This is not a cue bid of the ace of hearts. The trump ace can never be cue bid. If you need to know about the ace of trumps, the only way to find that out is by using Blackwood. Now put yourself in the North position.

(4)   Partner has announced that points are there for slam. Both clubs and spades have been cue bid; partner is obviously worried about diamonds. He has denied having the ace and you are looking at the KQ. You know that the opponents can't take the first two diamonds. Partner presumably has good hearts. He wouldn't likely be trying for a slam with bad diamonds, if he didn't have good trumps.

There are a few other points of slam bidding that you will want to know as you become more experienced. Minor suits can be a problem in slam bidding. Suppose you and your partner have agreed on clubs as the trump suit, as in the auction 1♣—3♣ and you know that there are enough points for slam. Suppose you bid 4NT with only one ace in your hand and partner answers with 5♦, showing one ace. It's too late for you to stop in 5♣. You might want to try 5NT as your only chance for a makeable contract, but if you bid that, partner will answer kings. A new suit by you, at this point, such as 5♡ or 5♠ requests partner to bid 5NT, which you will pass. Remember clubs were agreed upon as trumps, so a new suit on the five level can't be for play.

Another situation you can face is the following: partner opened 1♠ and you bid 3♠ with

♠ Q 10 5 3 2
♥ — — —
♦ K Q 8 2
♣ A 5 4 2

If partner now bids 4NT, you have a problem. You don't like to answer 5♦ as you have control of hearts as well as your ace, but if you answer 5♡ showing two aces, partner may get over-zealous and go for a grand slam because he thought you had two aces. (He may have a good heart suit and thinking you have the ace, he could count 13 tricks.) The best solution is to jump to six in your void (6♡) which shows one ace and a void in the suit in which you jumped. Partner will now bid 6♠ unless the heart void would be what he needed to bid 7♠. Be sure you don't jump in a void which is higher ranking than the agreed upon suit. If hearts were the suit agreed upon and partner bid 4NT, when you have 1 ace and a void in spades, a 6♠ bid by you would force partner to bid 7♡. In this situation, you respond to partner's 4NT bid with a bid of 6♡. This says that you have one ace and a void in a higher ranking suit, which in this case would have to be spades.

If you should have no aces and a void, it's usually best to simply show no aces (5♣). If you should happen to have two aces and a void, a grand slam should be a consideration if the hands appear to fit well.

QUIZ ON SLAM BIDDING

1. _____points will usually produce a small slam.
2. _____points will usually produce a grand slam.
3. If you bid Blackwood, a response of 5♡ shows_____ace(s), 5♣ shows_____ace(s), 5♠ shows_____ace(s) and 5♢ shows_____ace(s).
4. In the auction 1♡—3♡—4NT—5♢—5NT, what does 5NT mean?
5. South opens the auction with 1♡, North bids 3♡ and South then bids 4♣.
   What does 4♣ mean?
   Can the South hand have the ace of spades?
   Can the South hand have the ace of diamonds?
6. In the auction 1♡—2♠—3♠—4NT—6♢, what does 6♢ mean?
7. In the auction 1NT—4NT, is 4NT Blackwood?
8. In the auction 2♡—3♡—4NT—6♡, what does 6♡ mean?
9. In the auction 1♠—3♠—4♣—4♠, what does 4♣ mean? What does 4♠ mean?
10. In the auction 1♣—3♣—4NT—5♡, what does 5♡ mean?

XII

PREEMPTIVE BIDDING

A preemptive opening bid is a bid of three or more of a suit and is designed to interrupt the opponents' efforts to accurately bid to their best contract. It is made with a long good suit and very little strength outside that suit. The hand has fewer than 10 points in high cards. It is the modern style to have no aces or kings outside of the suit.

Suppose the opponents are vulnerable and you are non-vulnerable, and as dealer you have

♠ K Q J 9 7 5 3
♥ 4 3
♦ 8 2
♣ 7 3

An opening 3♠ bid might rate to be a very useful preempt. The reasoning is this: you have six tricks with spades as trumps; if partner has two tricks for you, such as the AK of clubs, you would only go down one trick; the opponents probably have a game. Your hand rates to take no tricks on defense as one of the opponents is likely to be short in spades. If partner's hand happens to be weak, and you are doubled, you may lose 500 points, but then the opponents surely have a game, which will give them 700 points for winning the rubber, and they could even have a slam. A small slam would be worth another 750 points if they had bid it. When you preempt, you rather hope partner is on the weak side and that the opponents fail to bid their game or bid a wrong game, or that partner has a big hand and that the opponents enter your auction and partner doubles and beats them a bunch. (Vulnerable doubled down three is 800 points!)

It is a real problem for a person with

♠ 6 4 3
♥ A 8 6 4 3 2
♦ A Q
♣ K Q

to know what to do when the person in front of him opens 3♠. This is the real bonus of preempting. It's not so much that you may save a few points if they miss their game, but they may bid an impossible game or slam or a wrong one when forced to make a decision at a high level.

Because of the fact that it's rather fun to be the cause of your opponents going wrong, the whole world seems to love to preempt. There's a bit of larceny in all of us. One of the bad things that could happen if you get too carried away with preempting is that your partner would not know what to expect. Partner could happen to be the person with the big hand.

For this reason, some guidelines need to be established as to what makes for effective preempts.

1. A GOOD SUIT OF AT LEAST SEVEN CARDS WITH A MINIMUM OF TWO HONORS, very little strength outside of the suit and less than 10 HCP in all. It is especially important to stick closely to this when partner is not a passed hand. He might have a good hand and needs to be able to rely on you for what you said you have. It is important to have neither more nor less.

2. AWARENESS OF VULNERABILITY.

Let's examine the first condition. You are the first to bid with the following hands:

1. ♠ A 7 6 5 4 3 2
   ♥ K 5 4
   ♦ 7 6
   ♣ 3

2. ♠ 4
   ♥ K Q J 7 6 5 2
   ♦ Q 7 5
   ♣ 7 4

3. ♠ A Q 8 7 5 4 2
   ♥ A 5
   ♦ 6 5
   ♣ 9 3

1. Your suit isn't good enough for a preemptive bid; you also have an outside K. Pass. You will have a chance to bid your spades later. The problem with preempting with hands that have defensive tricks is that, although you may have "stolen the bid," it is of no value because the opponents couldn't make anything.
2. This is a good 3♡ preempt.
3. This hand is too good to preempt. Although you have only 10 high-card points, your suit is good and with your outside A, it would be much better to open this hand 1♠.

The second important consideration in preempting is vulnerability. There are four conditions:
1. They are vulnerable—you are not. You need six tricks.
2. No one is vulnerable. You need six tricks.
3. Everyone is vulnerable. You need seven tricks.
4. You are vulnerable—they are not.

1. When preempting, you have to consider the consequences of your getting doubled. The most ideal time to preempt is in Case. 1. If you were to play in 3♡ doubled and you went down two, or even three, the opponents would receive 300-500 points. If, however, you botched their communications so that they missed a game, you prevented them from getting a 700 rubber. This would have been a well-timed preempt, if you had the right hand.
2. This is a fairly good time to preempt. If you were to preempt with 3♢, for example, and get doubled, down two would be -300. A non-vulnerable game is worth about 300 points when you consider the total picture of game bonus points, plus the trick scores which is another 100 points. If the opponents missed a game due to your preempt, you are ahead in the deal. With nobody vulnerable, you want to have six or seven tricks in your hand, so that you don't go down more than three, as doubled that's -500. That's a little more than their game is worth, but you may also cause them to miss a slam or cause them to bid the wrong game or slam, and you would then end up with a plus score.
3. This time is okay to preempt, but a little more caution is needed. If the opponents win the next game, it is worth 500 points plus the trick score. However, you are vulnerable also, so you want to be sure you have seven tricks in your own hand for a three-level preempt. If you had only six and were doubled, down three is -800 points. That's too much.

4. This is a very uninspired time to preempt. Only with an extremely distributional hand would you even consider it.

It is possible to preempt with a bid of four or five of a suit as well as a bid on the three level. This occurs less often as you need very long suits (eight or nine) for these bids. The same general conditions apply, i. e., good suit and little outside, and an awareness of vulnerability, so you know how much you are risking. With neither side vulnerable, you have

♠ A K J 7 6 5 3 2
♥ 7 6 3
♦ 4 3
♣ — — —

Open 4♠. You have a probable eight tricks in your own hand with spades as trump, so doubled you would be down two, or 300 points. It may cause the opponents to miss something or drive them into a contract that fails where another one would easily have made. You are putting pressure on your opponents, but because your suit is good, your own neck is not on the chopping block.

Once you have preempted, you have told your story. You should not bid again unless your partner forces you. If partner is an unpassed hand, a new suit below the game level would be forcing. After three passes, there is little merit in a preempt of the usual sort, as the opponents have had a chance to bid and didn't.

Once in a while, partner will preempt before you have had a chance to bid. With most hands, you will simply pass, but with hands that have enough *quick tricks* or quick winners, you will want to bid.

Quick tricks are tricks that you expect to take the first or second time a suit is led.

$$
\begin{array}{ll}
A & = 1 \\
AK & = 2 \\
AKQ & = 2 \\
KQ & = 1 \\
AQ & = 1\frac{1}{2} \\
K2 & = \frac{1}{2}
\end{array}
$$

When partner has preempted, add the tricks promised by partner to your quick tricks. If there are enough tricks for game, bid it. Let's take a classic non-vulnerable preempt by partner. Partner has opened 3♡ with

♠ 3 2
♥ K Q J 7 6 4 2
♦ J 7
♣ 6 5

1. ♠ K Q J 7 2   2. ♠ A 6 5 4
   ♥ 9 8   ♥ 8 5
   ♦ K Q 2   ♦ A 4
   ♣ K 3 2   ♣ A K 7 3 2

1. You have an opening hand, but only 2½ quick tricks. Partner has promised only six tricks. You should have 3½ quick tricks to bid 4♡. If you were vulnerable, you would need only 3 quick tricks as partner should promise seven tricks.

2. Bid 4♡. You have 4 quick tricks. It seems funny raising partner with only two cards, but when partner has announced a seven-card suit, two in your hand is good support. With enough quick tricks, a singleton in partner's suit would be adequate.

PREEMPTIVE BIDDING QUIZ

1. A preemptive bid on the three level should have ____ or more cards of the suit.
2. A vulnerable preempt would guarantee ____ tricks.
3. A nonvulnerable preempt would guarantee ____ tricks.
4. The most advantageous time to preempt is when the opponents are ____ and you are ____.
5. In responding to a preempt, ____ are the important considerations.
6. An AK is ____ quick trick (s).
7. An AQ is ____ quick trick (s).
8. A KQ is ____ quick trick (s).
9. A K32 is ____ quick trick (s).
10. An AJ2 is ____ quick trick (s).

With all vulnerable, what do you bid with the following hands? You dealt.

11. ♠ K J 10 8 7 4 2
    ♥ 8 6 2
    ♦ 6 3
    ♣ 7

12. ♠ K Q J 9 7 5 3
    ♥ A J 7
    ♦ 8 2
    ♣ 3

13. ♠ K Q J 7 5 3 2
    ♥ 3
    ♦ Q J 10
    ♣ 6 4

14. ♠ A 3
    ♥ 2
    ♦ K Q J 10 7 6 4
    ♣ K 5 2

With all nonvulnerable, your right hand opponent has passed, what do you bid?

15. ♠ K Q 10 8 7 3 2
    ♥ Q J 7
    ♦ 5 4
    ♣ 5

16. ♠ A Q 7 6 4 3 2
    ♥ K Q 3
    ♦ 4 3
    ♣ 5

17. ♠ J 9 8 7 5 3 2
    ♥ A K 2
    ♦ 7 5
    ♣ 2

18. ♠ 3 2
    ♥ 2
    ♦ K Q J 10 7 6 4
    ♣ Q 5 2

Your partner opens 3♡, the next person passes, and no one is vulnerable.

19. ♠ A K Q 7 6 5
    ♥ 6 5
    ♦ J 10 2
    ♣ 5 4

20. ♠ A K 3
    ♥ 6 5
    ♦ A 7 6 5
    ♣ K Q 4 3

21. ♠ K Q 6 5 2
    ♥ A
    ♦ Q J 7 6
    ♣ Q J 5

1. 7
2. 7
3. 6
4. Vulnerable, nonvulnerable
5. Quick tricks
6. 2
7. 1½
8. 1
9. ½
10. 1
11. Pass. A preempt would be too risky. You have only five or six tricks.
12. Bid 1♠. This is too good a hand to preempt.
13. Bid 3♠. You have a likely seven tricks, six spades and one diamond.
14. Bid 1♢.
15. Bid 3♣.
16. Bid 1♠. This is much too good to preempt.
17. Pass. Your suit is bad and you have too much outside.
18. Bid 3♢.
19. Pass. You have a good suit, but not enough quick tricks for game.
20. Bid 4♡. You have 4 quick tricks.
21. Pass. You have a good hand, but only 2 quick tricks.

XIII

IT IS YOUR LEAD

There are many different conditions to consider when making the opening lead. You might be defending NT or a suit contract, partner may not have bid, there may be an unbid suit, an opponent may have bid your best suit, you may be defending a partial or a slam, etc. This chapter will cover standard leads with some explanations given as to the logical reason for the lead.

Leading against NT contracts

Suppose your opponents had a simple auction of 1NT-3NT. Your objective is to defeat the contract. The best chance of accomplishing this is usually to establish a long suit, either in your hand or in partner's, as the opponents presumably have the bulk of the high cards. When partner has not bid, the normal lead is the fourth card down from your longest suit (K86<u>5</u>2), unless the suit contains a sequence, in which case you lead the top of the sequence. A sequence is defined as three or more touching cards of which the top card must be at least as big as a 10, e.g. J10942. J10842 is a near sequence and should be treated as a sequence. Lead the J with either of these suits. There are two reasons for leading the top of a sequence rather than fourth best. First, the high cards should be good enough to drive out the opponents' top honor(s) without having to give up more tricks than necessary. Suppose you have QJ1074 of a suit you have chosen to lead and declarer has AK9. Your Q and J could drive out the A and K and your 10 could capture the 9. By that time, your two remaining cards would probably be good as everyone else would likely be out of the suit. Had you lead fourth best, however, declarer would win a trick with the 9 as well as the A and K. The other reason for selecting the top of a sequence is to let partner know something about what you have. When you hold the QJ10 of a suit, they are all the same size as far as their trick taking potential. If you consistently lead the Q with this holding, partner will know what to expect.

The following are examples of suits you have chosen to lead versus a NT contract. The underlined card is the standard lead.

1. A86<u>5</u>2	2. K75<u>3</u>	3. <u>Q</u>J1032	*4. AK4<u>3</u>2	5. <u>Q</u>J862
*6. KJ<u>1</u>094	*7. <u>Q</u>J962	*8. A<u>K</u>Q42	9. QJ<u>7</u>4	*10. K98<u>7</u>2

⋆4. If you play an honor first followed by a low card, partner would be unable to return your suit if he started out with a doubleton.

⋆6. Lead the top of your interior sequence.

⋆7. This is close enough to a sequence to treat it as such.

⋆8. You hope for this suit to run. The lead of the A against NT is reserved as a special request for partner to drop an honor, such as when you have AKJ109.

⋆10. The 9 is not the top of an inside sequence. A sequence must contain an honor.

Sometimes you will elect to lead from a bad suit. This will most commonly occur when you have a bad hand, when the opponents have bid your best suit, or when your hand has so many values that partner rates to be broke.

Suppose you have

♠	K	J	9	3 2
♥	8	3	2	
♦	4	2		
♣	6	5	2	

and your RHO opens with 1♠ and later becomes the declarer in 3NT. You do not want to lead a spade into declarer's bid suit, and you have no other suit of your own. If you should decide to lead a heart, you don't want to lead low and cause partner to think it's your best suit. You should lead the 8. This type of lead is referred to as the "top of nothing". Partner can almost always tell by looking at his own hand and the dummy whether or not you led fourth best or the top of nothing. If, for example, he sees the QJ6 in dummy and he has A954 in his hand, he will know it wasn't fourth best as the only two cards you could have bigger than the 8 would be the K and 10.

Defending against 6 or 7 NT, a passive lead of the top of nothing or the top of a sequence is preferred to low from an honor. If you have an honor, partner rates to have little or nothing. You don't want to give away a trick as it could give declarer the extra trick he needs to make the slam.

If partner has bid, it's wise to lead his suit unless you have a very good reason for doing otherwise. Partners have a way of becoming very unhappy when they have bid and you select a more "imaginative" lead. In the following examples, partner has bid this suit and it's your lead, (or it could be an unbid suit and you are hoping it is partner's suit).

*1. K3<u>2</u>   *2. <u>A</u>2   *3. <u>K</u>2   *4. <u>9</u>3   5. A6<u>5</u>   *6.QJ3   7. Q64<u>2</u>

★1. It is best to lead low from this holding. Declarer may have Q65 and you could capture the Q with your K if you led low.

★2-3-4. When you lead from a doubleton, the upper card is the standard lead against any contract.

★6. This is not a sequence as it's only two cards, but with only three cards of which two are honors, it is often necessary to get them out of your hand early, so that the lead doesn't end up in your hand rather than in partner's. You could "block" the suit if you don't lead the Q.

Leading against suit contracts

When there is a trump suit, the non-trump suits will often be trumped the the third time the suit is played, so your object is not to establish a suit, but to take a trick or two before declarer or dummy is out. If partner is short, you may be able to create a ruff for him.

From touching honors, two or more, lead the upper, except from the AK, lead the K. From most other suits lead fourth best as in NT. An exception is a suit containing an ace. Usually suits headed by the A without the K should be avoided as an opening lead in that you hope to capture opponents' honors with your aces. However, when you have a long suit, five or more, or a short suit, it may work well to lead the A. It is very dangerous to underlead an A, (that is to lead low when you have the A), because if declarer or dummy has a singleton K, you will be left clutching your A. Sometime people say that you should not underlead a K. That is not valid, but there is a good deal of validity in not underleading aces, against a suit contract.

Examine the standard leads with these suits versus a trump contract.

*1.	KQ832	2.	K853	3.	A97432	4.	QJ832
5.	AK652	*6.	A3	7.	92	8.	Q863
*9.	K83	10.	832	*11.	8732	12.	QJ74
13.	J8752						

★1. Lead the upper from touching honors. Against NT you would lead fourth best.

★6. In this case you lead the A followed by the 3, in hopes of getting a ruff.

★9. Note the lead of the 3. The K is a standard lead from KQ, AK or occasionally from K doubleton, but when you have a K with small cards, you should lead low.

★11. Some texts say to lead fourth best from four or five small, but the advantage of leading the top from a bad suit is that when partner gains the lead he will know whether or not he should bother to return that suit or look for something better. A lead of a low card suggests that you have an honor.

QUIZ ON IT IS YOUR LEAD

Assuming this is the suit you have chosen to lead, which card do you lead? In the first blank write your lead against NT, in the second against a suit contract.

1.	KQ862	11.	7642	1. __ __		11. __ __	
2.	Q642	12.	KJ64	2. __ __		12. __ __	
3.	J10932	13.	10832	3. __ __		13. __ __	
4.	AK632	14.	AKQ42	4. __ __		14. __ __	
5.	A86432	15.	K10983	5. __ __		15. __ __	
6.	KJ1093	16.	K9872	6. __ __		16. __ __	
7.	832	17.	A6	7. __ __		17. __ __	
8.	J864	18.	KQJ62	8. __ __		18. __ __	
9.	QJ42	19.	76	9. __ __		19. __ __	
10.	Q42	20.	J10732	10. __ __		20. __ __	

Review this quiz sheet often until your leads become almost second nature.

Choose the card you would lead from these holdings, assuming partner has bid this suit. In the first blank write your lead against NT, in the second against a suit.

21.	K32	26.	982	21. __ __		26. __ __	
22.	A32	27.	J4	22. __ __		27. __ __	
23.	QJ3	28.	Q63	23. __ __		28. __ __	
24.	K3	29.	10862	24. __ __		29. __ __	
25.	104	30.	K742	25. __ __		30. __ __	

Answers to quiz

1. 6,K 2. 2,2 3. J,J 4. 3,K 5. 4,A 6. J,J 7. 8,8 8. 4,4 9. 2,Q 10. 2,2 11. 7,7 12. 4,4 13. 2,2 14. K,K 15. 10,10 16. 7,7 17. A,A 18. K,K 19. 7,7 20. 3,J 21. 2,2 22. 2,A 23. Q,Q 24. K,K 25. 10,10 26. 9,9 27. J,J 28. 3,3 29. 2,2 30. 2,2

XIV

BASIC SUIT COMBINATIONS

When looking at a suit and trying to determine how many possible tricks to expect, it is helpful to visualize possible cards in the opponents' hands and to have some awareness of the most likely holdings that could exist. With a combination of study and experience, one can become very good at this.

If you have had little experience with cards, it would be very helpful to take one suit out of a deck and lay out each combination as you read it. Deal the remaining cards of the suit to your opponents. You are the declarer, South, in a NT contract and you want to take the number of tricks listed. You won the previous trick in your own hand, but have plenty of entries in dummy, should you choose to lead from there.

Note: WHEN YOU ARE PLANNING THE PLAY OF A SUIT, IT IS NOT NECESSARY TO HOPE THAT AN OPPONENT *PLAYS* A PARTICULAR CARD, ONLY THAT HE *HAS* THAT CARD.

1.	AQ	2.	AKJ	3.	A32	4.	Q54
	2 tricks		3 tricks		3 tricks		2 tricks
	432		2		QJ10		A32

1. If you want to win two tricks with this suit, play low toward the AQ and if your LHO plays low, play the Q. If the K is on your left, the Q will be a winner. This is not an attempt to deceive your opponents. If your LHO has the K, he is helpless. If he plays low, your Q wins; if he plays the K, you play the A and your Q is now good. This is called a finesse. You will win two tricks any time the K is on your left, which is half of the time.

2. There are two sure tricks. If you need to take three tricks, lead low towards your J. If LHO plays low, play the J and "hope" the Q is on your left. This is basically the same situation as #1.

3. Lead the Q hoping the K is on your left. If LHO plays low, you play low. If this wins, you next play the J, again playing low if the K is not played. Notice if you lead the Q and the K is played, you would win the A and your J and 10 are now winners. Once again, you don't care whether or not your LHO plays the K or not, as long as he has the K you are assured of three winners.

4. This looks like example #3, but is very different. If you were to play another suit to get the lead in the North hand, so you could lead the Q, it would accomplish nothing. If your RHO covered your Q with the K, you would win the A and be left with what you started with, one trick. If the K was on your left, that would be no better. Leading the Q gains nothing, unless the opponents make an error. If, however, you try to visualize a holding that would legitimately give you a second trick in this suit, you should lead the 2 towards your Q and hope the K is on your left. If your LHO plays low, you will proceed on your assumption, or "hope", and play the Q. If, when you led the 2, your LHO played the K, you would lose this trick, but your Q would now be a trick when you regain the lead.

The play of a suit combination is often the same in NT as it is in a trump contract. In this next set, the examples could be a suit you are playing in a NT contract, or it could be the trump suit. In either case, you are trying to win all of the tricks with this suit. You won the opening lead in your hand (South) and are now ready to play this suit.

5. AJ54	6. AJ542	7. AKJ2	8. AJ32
K632	K873	10964	Q654

5. Play the K and next lead low towards the AJ. If left hand opponent plays low, finesse the J. The finesse works more often than playing for the Q to fall under the A. Notice that playing the A, then leading the J is a totally losing play, as you don't have the 10. If the Q is on your right, your opponent will play the Q and you will be left with no chance to win all the tricks.

6. With nine cards, missing the Q, play the K and if both follow, it is slightly better to play the A than to finesse the J.

7. In this case you should finesse by leading the 10 and playing low if it is not covered with the Q. If, however, you have plenty of entries in other suits, you could play the A first, then come back to your hand to lead the 10 for a finesse. This gives you the added chance of a singleton Q on your right.

8. Before reading on, see if you can figure out how to play this suit in order to take all four tricks. There is only one holding that permits this . . .

   Lead low towards the AJ and finesse the J. If this wins, play the A. If the K was doubleton on your left, you will win all four tricks as the Q would now pick up the outstanding card. If you were to lead the Q and it was covered, you could win the A and play the J, but that's only two tricks. Which ever opponent started out with three cards would now win the next trick with the 10 or the 9.

In the next group you are in a NT contract, or you are in a trump contract and this is one of your suits other than trump. You are South and you won the previous trick in your hand. You want to take the number of tricks listed.

	KQ2	854	AJ10	AQ10
	9.	10.	11.	12.
	2 tricks	1 trick	2 tricks	3 tricks
	432	Q32	432	432

9. Lead towards the KQ2. If LHO plays low, play either the K or Q. If it loses to the A, you have only one winner, but if the A is on your left, you will win two tricks by coming back to your hand and leading towards the other honor. Assuming plenty of entries outside of this suit, you will win two tricks half of the time. Once again you don't need to hope that your LHO plays the A, you only hope he has it. You can't control what the opponents do.

10. This is a dismal suit to try to depend on for a trick, but once in a while your bidding may have been something less than brilliant. If you are counting probable winners with this suit, it is zero. If you must take a trick with this suit, your best bet is to lead towards your Q twice, playing for both the A & K to be on your right. This example is listed only because people often look at this as a likely trick and this combination will rarely produce one.

11. With this suit you should plan to take two finesses. Lead low from your hand, playing the 10 if LHO plays low. If this loses to the K or Q, return to your hand with another suit and lead toward the AJ and if LHO plays low, repeat the finesse by playing the J. This wins two tricks when the K & Q are split, i.e., one in each of the opponents' hands, and when both the K & Q are held by your LHO. Your chances are very good of winning two tricks with this holding.

12. This is similar to the last example. Lead low and if LHO plays low, play the 10. If it loses to the K, you now have two tricks. If it loses to the J, come back to your hand and repeat the finesse. You play the 10 first rather than the Q because if both the K & J are "onside", you can win all three tricks. If your LHO has them both, he is caught. It would do him no good to play one of them, because if he played the J you would win with the Q and would have the A10 left over his K.

With some combinations it is advantageous to have the opponents lead the suit for you. It is sometimes possible that they will, if you can avoid playing the suit. In the next set, notice which combinations you would like to have led for you, if there were a choice.

13.	AJ2	14.	A2	15.	J32	16.	Q762
	K103		Q3		Q64		J543

13. If either opponent were to lead this suit, you would have three certain tricks simply by playing low from the next hand. If the third person to play plays the Q, you would win and you have the next two tricks. If the Q is not played your J or 10 would win and you still have the A & K. This is not a bad suit to have to play yourself, however. You have a two-way finesse. You could lead the 3 towards the AJ if you thought the Q was on your left, or get to dummy and lead the 2 towards your hand and play the 10 if you thought that the Q was on your right.

14. It is almost hopeless to win two tricks with this combination if you have to play it yourself. If either opponent leads it for you, it is quite possible to win two tricks. If LHO has the K and leads a low card of the suit, you would play low from dummy and "let it ride" to your Q. If RHO led a low card of the suit, you would hope he had led from the K and play your Q from your hand.

15. If you have to start this suit yourself, you will often end up with no tricks in the suit. The reason for this is that if you lead from your hand and play the J and it loses to the A or K, when you later lead from dummy and play your Q it may lose to the other honor. For you to win a trick in this suit, without the opponents making the error of playing their A or K when you lead towards the J, you would have to play for one opponent to have started with both the A & K. If, however, the opponents were to lead this suit for you, you have a certain trick by playing low from the next hand. If the third hand plays the A or K, your remaining Q and J will create a certain trick with only one-higher honor left to drive out.

16. This suit would be nice to have an opponent lead for you. The opponents have five cards. The normal break is three in one hand and two in the other. If you have to lead it yourself, suppose you begin by leading low towards the Q and it loses to the K, when you next get the lead, say in dummy, lead towards your J. If your RHO plays small, your best bet is to play small hoping for

Q762

A9   K108

J432

You will be faced with thousands of different suit combinations. Those listed in this chapter are some of the common examples which will be very helpful to know. However, the most important reason for studying the examples carefully is that it will help you develop a logical approach to each situation.

XV

DECLARER PLAY IN NO TRUMP CONTRACTS

When you are playing a hand in a NT contract, count your winners before you begin to play. After the opening lead is made, look at dummy and your own hand and count the sure tricks, which you could take without having to lose any tricks. If your "top" tricks are not enough to make your contract, which will usually be the case, look for other possibilities for developing the extra tricks needed.

♠ A 2
♥ K Q J
♦ Q J 3 2
♣ 5 4 3 2

THE AUCTION

South	West	North	East

♠ K 3   1NT   pass   3NT   pass
♥ 10 9 8   pass   pass   pass
♦ A K 8 5
♣ K Q J 10   Opening lead—5 of spades

You are declarer with the South hand. The very first thing to do is count your top tricks. There are two spades and four diamonds which totals six top tricks. The reason for this careful count is to help you analyze what you need to make your contract. You need three more tricks. After winning the opening lead in your hand or in dummy, (either is okay), you need to play clubs immediately. After you lose to the ace, you will have three sure winners in clubs, which will give you nine tricks. It's very important that you play clubs while you still have a spade winner or "stopper".

If you have to lose a trick to make your contract, do so while you still have stoppers in the other suits.

If you made the error of playing your other spade winner before leading clubs, when the opponents won the ace of clubs, they could take enough spade tricks to defeat the contract. It would also be an error to play a heart at trick two. The opponents could win the ace and play another spade. The heart suit would not provide enough winners to make nine tricks.

Count your top tricks in each of the following suits.

1. AK2	2. AQ	3. AK3	4. AQJ32	5. AKQ2	6. AKQ2
QJ10	32	QJ1042	K65	8653	654

1. This is unfortunate. You have all five honors and can only take three tricks, as you have only three cards in each hands.
2. One sure trick.
3. Five sure tricks.

4. Four sure tricks, but this holding will almost always take five tricks as there are only five cards missing. The only time this combination wouldn't produce five tricks is if all five missing cards were in one opponent's hand. Count this as five probable winners.

5. Three sure tricks. This suit is favored to take four tricks. You have eight cards. If the missing five are divided three in one hand and two in the other, the opponents would be out after three top leads. The five cards will divide 3-2 a little better than two-thirds of the time.

6. Three sure tricks. You have seven cards of the suit. This suit will produce an extra trick if the opponents' cards divide perfectly, three in each hand. This will happen only a little over one-third of the time.

Point of play: When you are cashing tricks of a suit, play off the high honors in the hand that is short.
From example #3 in this chapter: A K 3
                                    Q J 10 4 2

Play the A & K, then lead the 3 to your QJ10. If you played the Q first, then the A & K, you could end up with the lead in dummy with two winners left in your hand. Sometimes you might have no outside entries. You can easily take five tricks in this suit without the use of another suit, by simply playing off your high honors in the hand that is short.
Another example: A Q 4 3 2
                      K 4

Play the K, then low to the AQ. If you play the A or Q first, then low to your K you would be stuck in the wrong hand and would have to depend on another suit for transportation.
Count your winners on the following hand.

♠ 5 4 3
♥ 5 2
♦ A 9 7 2
♣ A Q 7. 5

♠ 8 7 6
♥ A Q 6
♦ K Q J 3
♣ K 6 4

THE AUCTION

East	South	West	North
pass	1NT	pass	3NT
pass	pass	pass	

Opening lead—2 of spades

Assuming the opponents are leading fourth best, the opening leader doesn't have a five-card suit, so presumably the opponents cannot cash more than four spade tricks. You have eight top winners, one heart, four diamonds, and three clubs. Suppose the opponents do take four spade tricks and then switch to a diamond. What is your best play to make this hand? Work on it before reading on.

On the fourth spade you could discard a small diamond from dummy and a small heart from your hand. There are two possibilities for your ninth trick. This club suit could split 3-3, which would give you a trick with the 13th club, or the heart finesse could work. The clubs break 3-3 less than half of the time, but it doesn't cost to try it first, before finessing in hearts. If they don't break 3-3, you can still try the heart finesse. This gives you an extra chance to make your contract. Since this is not a situation where you need to drive out an honor, you should begin by playing the diamonds first; someone may discard a club from a four-card holding. It is this kind of playing that will help you make more of your contracts. Remember to do this planning before you play to the first trick. If you neglected to do your planning early and carelessly discarded a club from dummy on the fourth spade, you would have given up one of your chances.

						THE AUCTION			
♠	6 5 4								
♥	A 5 4								
♦	K J 7 5								
♣	7 6 3				South	West	North	East	

		South	West	North	East
♠	A Q	1NT	pass	2NT	pass
♥	7 3 2	pass	pass		
♦	A 8 3 2				
♣	K Q 5 2	Opening lead—8 of spades			

With the opening lead being a spade, you have five top tricks, two spades, one heart and two diamonds. Spades would normally be counted as one top trick, but with your LHO leading the suit, you are assured of two tricks. It is a "free" finesse. You need three more tricks to make your contract (2NT). Either the diamonds or clubs could provide two more. The diamond suit is longer, so that's a reasonable place to begin. Play the A and lead towards the KJ. If LHO plays low, finesse the J. Suppose the J wins but your RHO discards a club. You have found one extra diamond trick, but the suit didn't break well so two tricks are needed in clubs. Lead a club to the KQ and hope the A is on your right. If RHO plays low, play the Q. If this wins, go back to the dummy with the K of diamonds and lead another club. Notice that you shouldn't go to the board with a heart, because the opponents could then cash their hearts when they get in with the A of clubs.

North   The Whole Hand
♠ 6 5 4
♥ A 5 4
♦ K J 7 5
♣ 7 6 3

West   **East**
♠ K J 9 8 2   ♠ 10 7 3
♥ 10 9   ♥ K Q J 8 6
♦ Q 10 9 4   ♦ 6
♣ J 9   ♣ A 10 8 4

South
♠ A Q
♥ 7 3 2
♦ A 8 3 2
♣ K Q 5 2

Count your winners on the next hand.

```
♠  A  7  6
♥  A  K  Q
♦  A  Q  J  5                          THE AUCTION
♣  8  7  5
                      North      East      South      West
♠  Q  3  2            *1♦        pass      1NT        pass
♥  6  5  4            **3NT      pass      pass       pass
♦  4  3  2
♣  A  4  3  2         Opening lead—4 of spades
```

Bidding notes:

★North has 20 points—too much for a 1NT opener and not enough for a 2NT opener, so he opens 1◇, planning to make a strong rebid.

★★North knows that partner has 6-10 HCP. At the second bid, when there are enough points for game, he correctly goes right to game, since No Trump suits him fine.

You have six obvious tricks, but with this lead you can be sure of an extra spade trick by playing low from dummy. If the K is on the left, your Q will win this trick. If it is on your right, your Q will be a winner later. Two more tricks will be needed. Suppose you win the first trick with the Q of spades. What do you do next?

Your best bet is to hope the K of diamonds is "onside". You need to lead the diamonds right now as you have only one entry left to your hand and you may need to finesse diamonds twice. If the J of diamonds wins, come back to your hand with the A of clubs and lead towards the AQ, repeating the finesse.

Count your winners on the next hand.

```
♠  5  4
♥  A  Q  7  2
♦  K  8  7  5                          THE AUCTION
♣  A  J  2
                      South      West      North      East
♠  K  2                          1♦        pass       1♥        pass
♥  5  4  3            *1NT       pass      3NT        pass
♦  A  Q  J  4  3      pass       pass
♣  K  10  3           Opening lead—10 of diamonds
```

West apparently had no long suit that he wished to lead, so he selected the 10 of diamonds. There are five diamond tricks, two clubs and one heart, or eight top tricks. There is a possible extra trick in hearts or clubs, by finessing, or even in spades by leading towards the K. What is your safest way to find an extra trick? Think about this awhile before reading on.

Bidding note:

★The diamond suit is rebiddable, but 1NT is more descriptive as this hand is balanced and is a minimum opening hand. The 1NT rebid shows a balanced hand of 12-14 HCP.

You should win an early diamond trick on the board with the K and lead a club to the 10. The club suit could be finessed either way. Spades are your weakest suit, but cannot be attacked from the left without giving you a trick. If the finesse of the club 10 wins, you have nine tricks. If it does not, you have other chances. If the club 10 loses to the Q and LHO returns a club or a diamond (a spade return from your left would give you your nineth trick) you can try the heart finesse. If this loses to the K and a spade is returned, you can still hope for the spade A being on your right. This line of play gives you several choices. If you don't make it, you can complain loudly about your bad luck. You'll notice that you can make a lot of luck happen by good card play. Had you played a heart at trick two and lost the finesse of the Q, or played a club to the J and lost that finesse, you would run the risk of a spade through your K before you were able to try all of your possibilities. Your RHO is the one you're reluctant to have on lead, so you finesse the club so that if it loses, you can safely try another possibility.

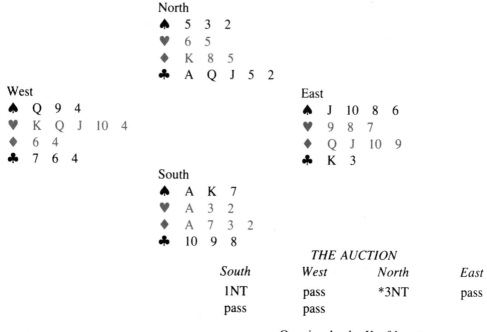

```
                        North
                        ♠  5  3  2
                        ♥  6  5
                        ♦  K  8  5
                        ♣  A  Q  J  5  2
West                                              East
♠  Q  9  4                                        ♠  J  10  8  6
♥  K  Q  J  10  4                                 ♥  9  8  7
♦  6  4                                           ♦  Q  J  10  9
♣  7  6  4                                        ♣  K  3
                        South
                        ♠  A  K  7
                        ♥  A  3  2
                        ♦  A  7  3  2
                        ♣  10  9  8
```

THE AUCTION

South	West	North	East
1NT	pass	*3NT	pass
pass	pass		

Opening lead—K of hearts

Bidding note:

★There is no need to bid this club suit. There are 10 HCP, which is enough for game. 3NT rates to be easier to make than five clubs, so forget the clubs and bid 3NT.

You have six top tricks with a club suit that could provide three or four more. The problem is if after winning the A of hearts you try the club finesse and it loses, the opponents may cash enough hearts to defeat you.

With some hands, you have no other choice but to rely on a finesse working, but with this hand, there is an extra chance available. There is no hurry in winning the A of hearts. In a NT contract, when the opponents lead a suit in which you are short, it is often good to "hold up" with the A until the third round. Now if the club finesse loses to the K, your RHO will be out of hearts and cannot return the suit. You will often hear people say "my finesses never work". These people are often ignoring the extra possibilities. Notice that when you do the club finesse, you can lead the 10 and play low from dummy, as when you have the Q, J, 10 and 9, they are effectively the same size.

North
- ♠ A J
- ♥ 6 5 4
- ♦ 6 4 3 2
- ♣ A K 7 2

West
- ♠ 6 5 4
- ♥ K Q J 8 7
- ♦ A Q 10
- ♣ 10 4

East
- ♠ 10 9 8 7
- ♥ 10 9
- ♦ 9 8 7
- ♣ 9 8 6 5

South
- ♠ K Q 3 2
- ♥ A 3 2
- ♦ K J 5
- ♣ Q J 3

THE AUCTION

South	West	North	East
1NT	pass	3NT	pass
pass	pass		

Opening lead—K of hearts

You have nine top tricks, four spades, one heart and four clubs. It's okay to hold up on the heart until the third round, but there is no need to with this hand, since you have nine sure tricks. Plan to cash your nine sure tricks. This hand has transportation problems. You need to be careful of your entries.

The spade suit must be started early as you can't cash four tricks without using another suit for entries. After winning the A of hearts, lead a small spade to the A & J; after playing both the A & J of spades, lead a low club to your J and cash the K & Q of spades, discarding small hearts from dummy. Now play your Q of clubs and then lead a low club to the A & K.

XVI

DECLARER PLAY IN A SUIT CONTRACT

Counting winners is effective in a NT contract. With the presence of a trump suit it is more effective to analyze a hand in terms of losers. **When playing in a trump contract, count losers before playing to the first trick.**

With most hands it is right to pull trump immediately. If you fail to do so, you may end up getting one of your winners trumped by the opponents. **When you are declarer in a trump contract, pull trump immediately unless you have a reason for needing to delay.** Inexperienced players lose more contracts by failing to pull trump than by pulling it too early.

♠	K	6	5	4
♥	6	5	4	
♦	A	4	3	2
♣	9	7		

THE AUCTION

East	South	West	North
pass	1♠	pass	2♠
pass	4♠	pass	pass
pass			

♠	A	Q	J	7	3
♥	7	3	2	
♦	K	Q	J	7
♣	A			

The opening lead—5 of diamonds

You have no trump losers, three heart losers and no losers in clubs or diamonds. Unless the opening lead is trumped on your right, this contract can easily be made. Assuming you win the diamond lead, play trump until the opponents are out. If you made the error of playing another diamond before removing trump from the opponents, someone would probably trump a diamond and you would have too many losers. When you have a good suit with as many cards in it as you have in diamonds and the opponent leads it, you should suspect a short suit lead. It obviously wasn't his good suit!

Practice counting your losers in the following suits. You are declarer in a trump contract and this is a side suit (non-trump suit). You have plenty of trumps in your hand and in dummy as well as plenty of entries. The suit in question was not led on the opening lead.

Dummy	1. A2	2. K4	3. QJ2	4. 654	5. A432	6. KJ2	7. 32
You	654	32	1064	Q82	K876	A64	AK4

Dummy	8. AQJ	9. 42	10. 5	11. AQ	12. KQ4	13. J54
You	432	AQ3	873	2	652	Q82

1. One loser. You can trump the third round in dummy.

2. One or two losers. You will lead low towards the K. If the A is on your left, you will lose one trick; if the A is "off side", you will lose two tricks.

3. Two losers.

4. Three likely losers. The Q will lose to the A or K the majority of the time.

5. The exact count won't be known until you play the suit, but with the usual break (3-2) you will have one loser.

6. One or no losers. You can lead towards the KJ for the finesse. Half the time you will lose no tricks and half the time you will lose one.

7. No losers. You can trump the 4 in the dummy.

8. One or no losers. If the K is "onside", you will lose no tricks by finessing twice.

9. One or no losers. You lead to the AQ. The finesse wins or it doesn't.

10. One loser. You can trump the rest.

11. No losers. Unless you need this suit to eliminate some other loser, you won't take the finesse, since you have no losers.

12. One or two losers. If the A is on your left, you will lose only one trick by leading toward the KQ, twice if necessary.

13. Two or three losers if you have to attack this suit yourself. This combination was listed in the chapter on suit combinations. There appears to be a trick, but in fact each of your honors will often be captured by the opponents' A & K.

Although it is usually right to pull trump early, there are some situations in which it is necessary to delay pulling trump. A careful count of losers will give you a guide as to what you need to do.

```
♠  8  6  4
♥  Q  J  4  2                    THE AUCTION
♦  J  3  2
♣  A  K  Q      North     East      South     West
                  1♣       pass       1♥       pass
♠  A  7  5        2♥       pass       4♥       pass
♥  K  10  7  5  3  pass     pass
♦  K  Q  10
♣  7  5                   Opening lead—K of spades
```

There is one trump loser, two spades, one diamond and no clubs. That is one too many losers. Having analyzed the problem, do you see a solution?

You need to play three rounds of clubs and discard a spade, which eliminates one of your spade losers. Had you played a trump at trick two, the opponents could win the A and cash two spades. It would be too late to make a useful discard on the clubs. The opponents would have three tricks and you can't avoid losing the A of diamonds.

Count your losers on the following hand

North
- ♠ 9 7 5
- ♥ 4
- ♦ Q J 10 5 3
- ♣ K 6 5 4

West
- ♠ 8 6 4
- ♥ K Q J 9
- ♦ A 8
- ♣ J 9 8 3

East
- ♠ 3 2
- ♥ 10 8 6 3 2
- ♦ K 7 6
- ♣ Q 10 7

South
- ♠ A K Q J 10
- ♥ A 7 5
- ♦ 9 4 2
- ♣ A 2

THE AUCTION

North	East	South	West
pass	pass	1♠	pass
2♠	pass	4♠	pass
pass	pass		

Opening lead—K of hearts

You have no trump losers, two diamond losers and no clubs. How about hearts? People often say that there are no heart losers because the small hearts can be trumped in dummy; then they proceed to pull trump. If you pull three rounds of trump, you will have no trump left in dummy with which to ruff the hearts, and you will lose two heart tricks. You need to delay pulling trump until you ruff the hearts.

Win the A of hearts and ruff a heart. Return to your hand with a trump and ruff the other heart. Now dummy is out of trumps, so return to your hand with the A of clubs and pull the rest of the opponent's trump. Now play the diamonds; you will lose only the AK of diamonds, making five.

When dummy has a short suit and only a few trumps, it is often necessary to delay pulling trump until you ruff the losers in dummy. This is the most common situation for needing to delay pulling trump.

```
        ♠  Q  6
        ♥  J  5  4
        ♦  A  K  8  6                    THE AUCTION
        ♣  9  8  4  3      South    West     North    East
                                     1♥     pass      2♥     pass
        ♠  5  3  2                    3♥     pass      4♥     pass
        ♥  A  K  Q  3  2   pass     pass
        ♦  7  5  3
        ♣  A  K                       Opening lead—2 of clubs
```

Count your losers. Probably none in the trump suit, one diamond, and two spades. That's three losers, which is okay. Do you see how to play this hand? What do you play after winning the club lead?

You are going to need to ruff one spade in dummy or you will lose three spade tricks. You must, therefore, lead a spade at trick two. If you played even one round of trump before playing spades, the opponents could thwart your plan by returning trump each time you lose a spade. Of course, the opponents could have ruined you had they led a trump at trick one, but the opponents can't always know what is the "killing" lead.

The last two examples are important because hands similar to them occur often. What actually happens by ruffing in the hand that has fewer trump is that you get an extention of your trump. Look again at this previous example.

```
                    North
                    ♠  9  7  5
                    ♥  4
                    ♦  Q  J  10  5  3
                    ♣  K  6  5  4

    West                                East
    ♠  8  6  4                          ♠  3  2
    ♥  K  Q  J  9                       ♥  10  8  6  3  2
    ♦  A  8                             ♦  K  7  6
    ♣  J  9  8  3                       ♣  Q  10  7

                    South
                    ♠  A  K  Q  J  10
                    ♥  A  7  5
                    ♦  9  4  2
                    ♣  A  2
```

By ruffing two hearts in the dummy, you actually take seven trump tricks, five in your hand and two in dummy. Notice that if you were to ruff a club in your hand, this would not extend your trump tricks. With some hands, if you deliberately set out to do trumping in the hand that is long in trumps, you can lose control. With this hand, you would still make it. It would cost you an overtrick. If you needed to make five, correct technique would be essential. The problem with ruffing clubs in your hand is that you would be out of trumps in both hands. When you get around to the diamond suit, you will be out of entries.

The expression "cross ruff" is one you will hear often, but the true cross ruff hand occurs rather seldom. It is nice to recognize it when it comes up, as it takes careful handling. The main characteristic is that each hand has a short suit with losers in the opposite hand that can be avoided only by ruffing.

♠ A J 5 2
♥ 9 7 5 4 3
♦ 2
♣ A 8 6

♠ K Q 10 3
♥ 2
♦ A 9 7 5
♣ K 5 3 2

The contract is 4♠. The opening lead is the K of hearts followed by the A which you ruff. If you were to play three rounds of trump, you would have only one trump left in dummy and none in your hand with which to ruff your losers. You have no side suit to use for discards. You would end up taking five trump tricks and probably only three other tricks, for down two.

Instead, you want to play this on a cross ruff, ruffing diamonds in dummy and hearts in your hand. The correct technique is to play off your side suit winners first, then begin the cross ruff. After ruffing the second heart, play off the A & K of clubs, then the A of diamonds, ruff a diamond, ruff a heart, ruff a diamond, etc. You rate to make five. Notice that the last several ruffs will be high trumps, so could not be over-ruffed. The reason for cashing the clubs early is to avoid giving the opponents a chance to discard clubs as you are cross ruffing and thus be able to trump your good clubs at the end of the hand.

Many consider defense to be the most difficult part of bridge. When you are declarer, you know your full arsenal, because partner's hand is visible. When you are defending you have to figure out what partner has. Defenders can transmit a great deal of information in the card play. It is unethical to give information by the manner in which you play, i.e., a big smile when you like partner's lead or a frown when you don't. However, there are socially acceptable ways of communicating this information. Tournament bridge has become rather sophisticated in defensive communications. However, to defend effectively on most hands, only a few tools are needed.

The first opportunity for partnership communication is the opening lead. The lead selected tells something about the suit led and sometimes about the rest of the hand. For example, after the opponents bid 1NT—3NT partner leads the 2 of spades. What do you know about partner's hand? You know that partner has no five-card suit, as presumably he would lead it if he had one. The 2 could not be from a five-card suit, if fourth best leads are used. This is one of the reasons why it is important to be accurate and consistent in the card selected for a lead.

When partner makes the opening lead, you will have an opportunity to communicate something about your hand at your first play. Suppose partner leads the 3 of hearts against a 4♠ contract and dummy has.

♠	A	4	3	2		Your heart suit is Q96.
♥	7	5	2			
♦	K	4	2			
♣	6	5	2			

You should play the Q of hearts, your highest card. This isn't so much to "tell" what you have, as to keep declarer from winning a trick cheaply. However, if your hearts were QJ6, you should play the J. When you hold touching honors, they are the same size as far as their trick-taking potential. The card you play is only to help communication. Suppose partner has led from K1083. If you play the J and declarer wins the A, partner will know that you have the Q. Do you see why? Surely declarer would not have used his ace if he could have won the trick with the Q. The play of the Q by you should deny holding the J. **When winning or potentially winning of a trick, play the lower or lowest of touching honors.** Notice that this is played the opposite from leading the suit. When on lead from QJ102 you would lead the Q, but if partner leads a low card in this suit and dummy plays low, you would play the 10, the lowest of your touching honors. This will help partner know when it is safe to continue a suit.

Look at the example again.

partner	dummy	you
	7 5 2	
K 10 8 3		Q 9 6
	declarer	
	A J 4	

Partner led the 3, dummy played small, you played the Q and declarer won the A. If partner gains the lead in another suit, he knows that cashing the K is likely to give declarer a trick since you denied having the J.

Another time you can communicate with partner is when he leads a high card against a suit contract. You can give your attitude towards the lead by the card you play. Suppose partner led the K of hearts against a diamond contract and your hearts are Q82. Partner presumably has the A. If the suit splits 4-3-3-3, you could take the first three tricks. You must urge partner to continue this suit by playing the 8. When he plays the A, you will play the 2. The "high-low" says that you like the lead. The high-low could be with smaller cards. If you had Q32, the 3 followed by the 2 would still be a high-low. You would also high-low with a doubleton if you wanted to ruff the next trick. However, if partner leads the K and you have the Q and a low card, do not play the Q, as it may be too valuable to waste. The play of the Q under the K would show either a singleton or some holding with both the Q and J.

In the next example, you are East defending against 3♠. The opponents have a game and a 30 partial. If they make this, they will win the rubber.

North
♠ Q J
♥ 5 3 2
♦ 10 7 4 3 2
♣ K J 5

West
♠ 5 4 3 2
♥ A K 8 6
♦ 9 8
♣ A 9 7

East
♠ K 6
♥ 9 7
♦ Q J 6 5
♣ 10 8 6 4 2

South
♠ A 10 9 8 7
♥ Q J 10 4
♦ A K
♣ Q 3

THE AUCTION

West	North	East	South
	pass	pass	1♠
pass	1NT	pass	2♥
pass	*2♠	pass	3♠
pass	pass	pass	

Opening lead—K of hearts

*With two honors in spades, North took a preference to spades since partner is known to have five spades and could easily be bidding a four-card heart suit.

Partner led the K, then A of hearts; you played the 9 & 7, and partner gave you a ruff. You have taken three tricks. Two more are needed. If you could get partner in again for another heart return, you could set the contract as you would be able to over-ruff dummy. Which suit do you try? Partner should have given a clue. When he returned the heart for you to ruff, he had two cards to lead back. There are two other suits, clubs and diamonds. If partner plays a high heart for you to ruff, it suggest leading a diamond back (the higher ranking suit); if he plays a low one, it suggests clubs (the lower ranking suit). Without this clue from partner you would be on a total guess. It takes some practice getting used to watching the small cards (spot cards), but it is not difficult.

Another situation to think about is when you win partner's opening lead and are considering which card to return. Partner leads the 5 of diamonds against 3NT. Dummy has the 9-8 and you have the AJ2. After winning the A, you need to return the J. The general idea is to get your high honors out of the way so that partner can run his long suit. Supposing the suit were

```
                                         9   8

             K   10   7   5   4      A   J   2

                         Q   6   3
```

If your were to return the 2 and declarer played the Q, partner could win the K, but now the suit is blocked. The whole suit is good, but the next play would put the lead in your hand. If you return the J, your side would take the first five tricks. **When returning partner's lead, the general rule is if you started with three, return the middle card; if you had four or more, return the fourth best.**

Partner has led a low card. After winning the A, return the card underlined. It would be the same if it were NT or a suit contract.

1. A9<u>2</u>   2. A85<u>2</u>   3. A<u>6</u>   4. A86<u>4</u>2   *5. A<u>J</u>102

★5. This is an exception to returning the fourth best. If you were defending against NT and partner has a five-card suit, you could block it if you don't get your J & 10 out of the way. Suppose declarer and dummy each had a doubleton and partner had K9752.

As a defender, when you are the last person to play, you should win the trick unless you have a specific purpose in refusing the trick. However, in second position when a low card is led, you should tend to play low unless you have a reason for playing a high card. Partner will still have a chance to win the trick. It is usually helping declarer if you prematurely play your honors on his low cards. The following example illustrates the point.

```
                   J   3   2

You
A   8   5          K   10   9   7

         Q   6   4
```

Declarer leads the 4. If you play your A declarer will eventually come to a trick with this suit. If you play low, partner can capture the J and later you can capture the Q and declarer will have no tricks.

When an honor is led, however, it is usually best to "cover" it. Usually, cover an honor with an honor unless you can see the next lower card in the hand that is leading it.

1.	Dummy			2.	Dummy			
	Q 3 2				Q J 10 2			
		You				You		
	K 8 6 4				K 8 6 4			

1. The Q is led from dummy. You should cover because you can't see the J. If declarer has some holding such as AJ4, when you cover the Q he will win the A and have one more trick with the J. If you don't cover the Q, the Q would win and declarer could win two more tricks with the AJ over your K, giving him three tricks instead of two.

2. There is no need to cover the Q since you can see the J, and there is no need to cover the J when you can see the 10. If you covered the Q you would gain nothing, but would give declarer an extra trick if he holds A doubleton, for example. Even worse is the sadness you would experience if partner had a singleton A.

The suggestion for second hand play and third hand play are not intended as rules. You will often hear people say "second hand low, third hand high, lead through strength, lead up to weakness" etc. etc. Bridge is a game of logic and cannot be learned by memorizing phrases. While there is some degree of truth to many of these statements, there are many exceptions. For example, it is seldom correct to refuse to take the setting trick, regardless of what seat you have.

The most effective defense begins when you can form a mental picture of the hands that you cannot see. This can be done in part by studying the dummy, remembering the bidding, and noticing partner's clues. Try it on this example.

Dummy (South)
♠ 8 3
♥ A 5 4
♦ 8 7 5 3
♣ A 6 4 2

THE AUCTION

West	North	East	South
pass	1NT	pass	2NT
pass	3NT	pass	pass
pass			

You
♠ 9 4
♥ 8 3 2
♦ 9 6 4 2
♣ K 9 5 3

Partner leads the Q of spades. There are a number of things that can be deduced about the unseen hands. Declarer should have 17-18 HCP. His opening bid showed 15-18, but he accepted the game invitation. The opponents have 25-26 HCP. You have 3 so partner has 11 or 12 HCP. You know that 3 of them are the Q & J of spades, so partner should have 8-9 additional points. Also, partner probably has five or more spades. You and dummy each have two so there are nine in the unseen hands. The opening bidder might have opened 1♠ if he held five of them. If you take a minute before playing to the first trick, you can deduce things of this nature. It is a habit that can be developed with relative ease.

Bidding starts with the number of tricks you hope to take over six. A bid of three is contracting for nine tricks.

For contracts bid and made the score is: Minor suits = 20 points per trick
   Major suits = 30 points per trick
   No Trump = 40 points for the first trick, 30 for each subsequent trick

GAME IS 100 POINTS OR MORE

Game bids vary depending on where the contract is played:

   5♣ or 5♢ (11 tricks) is game as 5 x 20 = 100 points
   4♡ or 4♠ (10 tricks) is game as 4 x 30 = 120 points
   3NT (9 tricks) is game as 40 + 30 + 30 = 100 points

The points recorded below the line record the contracts which are bid and made. There are various bonuses that can be made; they are recorded above the line.

Which ever side wins two games first wins what's known as a "rubber". The advantage of winning a rubber is that you receive 500 or 700 bonus points for this, 500 if the opponents have scored one game and 700 points if they have not.

Game can be scored all in one hand or part at a time. If on one hand you bid 3♢ and make three, you have 60 points (below the line). If on a later hand you bid 2♠ and take the eight tricks necessary, you score 60 more points below the line. 60 + 60 is greater than 100, so you have scored a game, part at a time. If, however, the opponents make a game after your 3♢ bid, but before your 2♠ bid, your partial no longer counts towards your game.

A SAMPLE RUBBER

	North/South WE		East/West THEY	
1. N/S bid 2♥, made 3.	4. 20			
2. E/W bid 3NT, made 3. E/W vulnerable.	1. 30		500	6.
3. N/S bid 1 NT, made 1.	1. 60		100	2.
4. N/S bid 3♣, made 4. N/S vulnerable.*	3. 40			
	4. 60			
5. E/W bid 4♠, made 4.				
6. Bonus points for winning rubber.			120	5.
	210		720	E/W won by 510 points

*Vulnerable means that you have won a game and are now in position to win the rubber if you win another game.

In the previous example, no one failed to make his bid. If one side fails to make their bid, the other side gets penalty points above the line. If the side that fails to make their contract has no game on in the current rubber, they lose 50 points for each trick that they are short. If they are vulnerable (a game scored) they lose 100 points for each short trick.

50 POINTS FOR EACH TRICK SHORT, NON-VULNERABLE

100 POINTS FOR EACH TRICK SHORT, VULNERABLE

A SAMPLE SCORE

WE		THEY	
			3.
		50	4.
3. 200		50	1.
		100	2.

1. N S bid 4♠ and took only nine tricks. Notice they got no credit for the tricks they took, since it was less than what they bid.
2. E W bid and made 5◇.
3. E W bid 5♣ and took only nine tricks.
4. N S bid 3♡ and took only eight tricks. Notice it's still only 50 points as N S still isn't vulnerable.

If a contract is doubled, meaning the opponents feel they can defeat the contract, the score is:

NON-VULNERABLE	VULNERABLE
100 for the 1st trick short	200 for the 1st trick short
200 for each one thereafter	300 for each one thereafter

If, however, a person does make a doubled contract, they get their trick scores doubled (2♡ doubled making would be 60 x 2 = 120 for tricks) plus 50 points above the line for the "insult". When the doubled trick score totals over 100, as in the case of 2♡ doubled, credit is also given for the game, even though it wasn't bid.

If a doubled contract is redoubled, the trick scores are doubled again; 1♡ doubled and redoubled is 120. The overtricks or undertricks count twice as much as doubled contracts. The insult remains 50 points if a redoubled contract is made.

OTHER BONUS POINTS

SMALL SLAM	500 points non-vulnerable
GRAND SLAM	1000 points non-vulnerable
SMALL SLAM	750 points vulnerable
GRAND SLAM	1500 points vulnerable

HOLDING 4 HONORS OF A SUIT YOU NAME AS TRUMP	100 points
HOLDING 5 HONORS OF A SUIT YOU NAME AS TRUMP	150 points
HOLDING ALL 4 ACES IN A NO TRUMP CONTRACT	150 points

GLOSSARY

AUCTION   the bidding

BLACKWOOD   a conventional bid of 4NT which asks partner how many aces he has

BOOK   the first six tricks taken by the declarer

CONTRACT   the final bid—(a double and redouble would be included as a part of the contract)

CONVENTION   an artificial bid which, by partnership agreement, asks a question or describes a particular type of hand, other than what is suggested by the bid itself.

DECLARER   the person within the partnership who first bid the suit (or NT) selected as the final contract. This person plays both his hand and the dummy.

DISTRIBUTIONAL POINTS   points given in the evaluation of a hand for doubletons, singletons, or voids

DOUBLE   a call made during the bidding which will increase the penalty points if the opponents fail to make their contract

DOUBLETON   a suit containing only two cards

DUMMY   the hand opposite declarer which is spread face up on the table during the play of the hand

FINESSE   an attempt to win a trick with a lower card when there is a higher card outstanding. (see sample hand at the end of Chapter II)

FORCING BID   a bid that partner should not pass at his next turn

GAME   scoring 100 points or more below the line. It can be accomplished part at a time (more than one hand) if the opponents don't bid a game in between.

HIGH CARD POINTS (HCP)   the value of a hand in terms of its high cards, A,K,Q,J.

HONORS   the A,K,Q,J,10 of a suit. In scoring, the points received for any one hand holding four or five of them in the trump suit or all four aces if the contracts is NT.

JUMP SHIFT   a deliberate one level jump to a new suit by responder or opener, for example, 1♡—2♠ or 1♢—1♡—2♠

LHO   left hand opponent

MAJOR SUITS   hearts and spades

MINOR SUITS   clubs and diamonds

NO TRUMP   a contract without a trump suit or a bid suggesting play without a trump suit

NON-VULNERABLE   the state of a pair which has not made a game in the current rubber

ONE-OVER-ONE BID   a bid of a new suit on the one level after partner has opened the bidding with one of a suit

OVERTRICKS   extra tricks taken after the contract has been fulfilled

OVERCALLS   a bid of a suit or NT after an opponent has opened the auction

PARTIAL or PART SCORE   bidding and making of a contract for which the score is less than 100 points

PREEMPTIVE BID   a high level bid which is intended to interfere with the opponents' auction by taking their bidding space. It is made with long suits and weak hands

QUICK TRICKS   high honors in a suit which are expected to win the first or second time the suit is led

REDOUBLE   a bid which increases again either the score for making the doubled contract or the penalty for failure to do so.

REVERSE   a second bid on the two-level or higher in a suit which is higher ranking than the first suit bid ($1\diamondsuit$—$1\spadesuit$—$2\heartsuit$)

RHO   right hand opponent

RUBBER   two game contracts made by one side

RUFF   to play a trump when unable to follow suit

SEQUENCE   three or more touching cards of which the highest is an honor

SET   to defeat a contract

SINGLETON   a suit containing only one card

SLAM   a bid of six or seven

SLUFF   to discard when out of the suit led

STAYMAN   a conventional bid of 2♣ after partner has opened 1NT. The bid is intended to ask opener if his hand contains a four-card major.

SUIT RANK   the order in which suits must be bid on the same level. The rank beginning with the lowest is clubs, diamonds, hearts and spades. No trump is higher ranking than any suit.

TAKE-OUT DOUBLE   a double which is intended as a request for partner to bid

TRICK   the four cards resulting after a card has been played from each hand. The highest card of the suit led wins the trick, unless it has been trumped.

TRUMP   a suit named as the master suit in the auction

TWO-OVER-ONE BID   responding on the two level with a new suit which is lower ranking than the one partner opened, for example 1♡—2♣.

VOID   holding no cards of a suit

VULNERABLE   the state of a pair which has made one game in the current rubber.

OTHER BOOKS BY NORMA SANDS
BRIDGE Mini Series

The Bridge Mini-Series is a series of award-winning booklets on 10 important topics.

$3.95 each
All 10 for $34.95

I. Fine Tuning Your Bridge
Minor suit openings, help suit game tries, judgment situations.

II. Later in the Auction
Responder's 2nd turn, opener's 3rd turn, reverses, after a 2 over 1 response.

III. Opening Leads Versus Suits
Analyzing the auction, leads to avoid, aggressive and passive leads.

IV. Double Trouble
Takeout, penalty and lead-directing doubles, redoubles, quiz.

V. Weak Two Bids
After partner opens, 3rd and 4th seat two bids, games and slams.

VI. Competitive Bidding
Overcalls at 1 and 2 level, Unusual NT, Michaels.

VII. Defensive Signals
Attitude signals, leads, count signals, suit preference.

VIII. Negative Doubles
After various level overcalls, related sequences.

IX. Slam Bidding I
Suit slams, quizzes, cue bidding, splinters.

X. Slam Bidding II
NT slams, 4 NT: Blackwood or quantitative?, Gerber, how aggressive to be.

BRIDGE HELPER $1.95
Summary of basic bidding, designed to accompany STANDARD AMERICAN BRIDGE UPDATE.

PLAYING THE CARDS $6.95
Subtitled "Developing Competence at the Bridge Table," this text spotlights techniques needed for winning plays.